Praise for

MY LEGS WERE PRAYING

"Amazing! Or Rose has accomplished the impossible—he has taken the complex story and teachings of one of the twentieth century's quintessential Jewish leaders and shared his life story and his essential beliefs in a way that will appeal and make sense to young readers. I know a lot about Heschel, but this book is so full of detail about his life and clarity about his beliefs, I learned more." —**Ruth Messinger**, global ambassador, American Jewish World Service

"In this beautiful new biography, Rose brings Rabbi Abraham Joshua Heschel's story, indeed his inner light, to life for a new generation. Now more than ever, we need everyone to know that faith can be a source of inspiration for individuals, and a bridge of cooperation between diverse communities. This book shows us how this was the case for Rabbi Heschel, and how it might be the case for each of us too." —**Eboo Patel**, founder and president, Interfaith America

"Or Rose has once again captured the brilliant spirit of Rabbi Heschel and shared it with an audience who desperately need Heschel's prophetic wisdom. Today's world is desperate for a model of living in pursuit of justice and peace. Heschel offers a path. Or Rose is a fabulous guide." —**Peter A. Geffen**, founder and president, The KIVUNIM Institute; founder of the Abraham Joshua Heschel School in NYC

"In powerful prose, *My Legs Were Praying* brings to life the legacy and profound moral witness of Rabbi Abraham Joshua Heschel. This compelling biography is a must read and serves as needed inspiration to embrace Rabbi Heschel's lifelong commitment to loving kindness and justice." —**Rev. Adam Russell Taylor**, president, Sojourners

MY LEGS WERE PRAYING

A BIOGRAPHY OF
ABRAHAM JOSHUA HESCHEL

RABBI OR N. ROSE
WITH RABBI DOV PERETZ ELKINS

FOREWORD BY
DR. SUSANNAH HESCHEL

AFTERWORD BY
AMBASSADOR SUZAN JOHNSON COOK

MONKFISH
BOOK PUBLISHING COMPANY
RHINEBECK, NEW YORK

Paperback ISBN 978-1-958972-72-4
eBook ISBN 978-1-958972-73-1

Library of Congress Cataloging-in-Publication Data

Names: Rose, Or N., author. | Elkins, Dov Peretz, author.
Title: My legs were praying : a biography of Abraham Joshuah Heschel / Rabbi Or N. Rose with Rabbi Dov Peretz Elkins ; foreword by Susannah Heschel ; afterword by Ambassador Suzan Johnson Cook.
Description: Rhinebeck, New York : Monkfish Book Publishing Company, [2025] | Includes index.
Identifiers: LCCN 2025000270 (print) | LCCN 2025000271 (ebook) | ISBN 9781958972724 (paperback) | ISBN 9781958972731 (ebook)
Subjects: LCSH: Heschel, Abraham Joshua, 1907-1972. | Rabbis--United States--Biography. | Jewish scholars--United States--Biography. | Civil rights workers--United States--Biography. | Selma to Montgomery Rights March (1965 : Selma, Ala.)
Classification: LCC BM652 .R58 2025 (print) | LCC BM652 (ebook) | DDC 296.3092 [B]--dc23/eng/20250129
LC record available at https://lccn.loc.gov/2025000270
LC ebook record available at https://lccn.loc.gov/2025000271

Book and cover design by Colin Rolfe

Monkfish Book Publishing Company
22 East Market Street, Suite 304
Rhinebeck, NY 12572
(845) 876-4861
monkfishpublishing.com

CONTENTS

We dedicate this book to the memory of our beloved teacher, colleague, and friend,
Rabbi Dr. David Ellenson
(1947-2023)
—a lover of the Jewish people and of humanity.
May the memory of the righteous be a blessing.
"Lovingkindness will stand firm forever."
Psalm 89:3

FOREWORD

My father loved being a father. And he was a wonderful father. When I remember him, I think most of all about his tenderness and his exuberance. He was full of affection, and he loved to show it. When I was little, he invented games for me, played "zoo," and even tried to take an interest in my paper dolls. As I grew older, he was my source of comfort and understanding, sympathizing with the pains of adolescence. Whenever he came home from his office, or I interrupted him while he was working, he threw open his arms and exclaimed, "Susie!"

Joy and excitement filled our home as soon as my father came home from work. He was anxious to share the news of his day, ready to play hide-and-seek with me, enthusiastic for the dinner my mother had prepared. After dinner, we frequently played "school" in the living room, with my parents pretending to be the pupils, while I was the teacher. We had a hilarious reenactment of my day at school, and my father loved to take the role of one of the mischievous little boys in my class.

My parents created a home imbued with the spirit that my father describes in his books. The Sabbath and Jewish holidays were days of celebration, but also times of holiness. We sometimes had guests for dinner, or for tea on *Shabbos* (Sabbath) afternoons, and the conversations inevitably turned to memories of Europe. Nearly all my parents' friends were refugee scholars from Europe, and years after the Second World War, they remained in shock at what had happened. Other times, my father would talk about Hasidic *rebbes* (masters), telling us stories and teachings of his ancestors.

My father's legacy is enormous. To scholars, he has given remarkable insights into Jewish thought, to religious people he has given a language to communicate across divisions. To me, as his only child, he gave a vision of the extraordinary heights of love and compassion a human being can reach.

Susannah Heschel, PhD
Eli Black Distinguished Professor of Jewish Studies
Dartmouth College

INTRODUCTION

"Let justice roll down like waters, and righteousness like a mighty stream."
—Amos 5:24
(English translation by A.J. Heschel, *The Prophets*, 1962)

On March 21, 1965, the Reverend Dr. Martin Luther King Jr. and other Civil Rights organizers led approximately 8,000 protesters on a fifty-four-mile march from Selma to Montgomery, Alabama. After completing their three-day trek along highway Route 80, these brave souls were joined by more than 15,000 demonstrators from across the country at the Alabama State Capital. The marchers took to the streets demanding that local government officials allow African Americans the opportunity to vote. Although the U.S. government had extended this right to Black people long ago, there were still many racist politicians and policemen stopping them from registering to vote in Southern states.

In fact, this was the *third* time in less than a month that Civil Rights leaders attempted to carry out this demonstration. Their first march on Sunday, March 7, is known as "Bloody Sunday" because of the brutality of the state police, who assaulted the peaceful protestors with clubs and tear gas as they attempted to cross the Edmund Pettis Bridge. Two days later, Dr. King led an abbreviated march and prayer service on that same bridge. While "Turn-Around Tuesday" did not end in violence, that evening four local white supremacists attacked three ministers (also white) from out-of-state, who had traveled to Selma to join the protest. Tragically, one of these individuals, Reverend James Reeb, died from his injuries.

With great sorrow, frustration, and determination, Dr. King and his associates planned a third march. They invited a distinguished group of national religious figures to join them in the front lines. One of these individuals was Rabbi Dr. Abraham Joshua Heschel. Dr. Heschel was a gifted Jewish scholar, teacher, and speaker, whose recent book, *The Prophets* (1962)—a detailed study of the ancient biblical champions of justice and mercy—was a source of great inspiration to Dr. King and other Civil Rights leaders.

As Heschel walked arm-in-arm with his colleagues, he was easy to spot in the crowd: He was a short, stocky man with flowing white hair, a bushy beard, who wore a dark *yarmulke* (Jewish head covering). Like the prophets of old, Heschel believed that standing up for others—particularly the most vulnerable members of society—is a sacred obligation. As he wrote, the religious person must seek to hold God and humankind "in one thought at one time," suffering "harm done to others," making "compassion" one's "greatest passion."

Heschel first learned these essential values as a child in Eastern Europe.

1

THE HESCHEL HOME

"I was very fortunate in having lived as a child in an environment where many people showed great compassion and understanding for other people."
—*The Eternal Light* television interview, 1972

Abraham Joshua (Avraham Yehoshua) Heschel was born on January 11, 1907 (Hebrew date: 25 *Tevet*), in Warsaw, Poland. He was the descendent of eight generations of Hasidic *rebbes* ("rabbis" or masters)—spiritual teachers and guides who led Jewish communities throughout Eastern Europe. The Hasidic masters were famous for their use of storytelling, music, dance, and improvisational teaching to inspire and instruct their communities. Abraham Joshua's father, Rabbi Moshe Mordechai, was a rebbe; his mother, Rivka Reizel, was the daughter and the twin sister of rebbes; Abraham Joshua's parents expected that he, too, would become a Hasidic master one day.

Abraham Joshua was the youngest of six children. He had four sisters: Sarah Brakha, Esther Sima, Gittel, and Devorah Miriam; and one brother, Jacob (Ya'akov). As the baby, he was pampered, fussed over, and teased by his siblings.

The Heschels lived in a small apartment attached to a *shteibel* (small prayer house and study hall) at 40 Muranowska Street, in the heart of Hasidic Warsaw. This was where his father served as a rabbi, teaching the members of his community the wisdom of the Jewish tradition, and guiding them in their day-to-day lives.

Rabbi Moshe Mordechai was the leader of a very poor community and was paid only a small salary. Rivka Reizel was responsible for the care of her children and for the upkeep of the Heschel home.

Heschel's father, Rabbi Moshe Mordechai Heschel,
and his mother, Rivka Reizel Heschel
(Courtesy of Yitzhak Meir Twersky and Thena Heshel Kendall)

Life was not easy for the Heschels. Nonetheless, their home was a place of love and warmth. For example, the Heschels had a beautiful family *tzedakah* (support for the needy) tradition: every night after dinner, they gathered any money left in the apartment, and Abraham Joshua's father gave it away to the poorest people in the neighborhood. This practice was based on the simple conviction that to call oneself a "Hasid" requires a person to express their piety (religious dedication, *hasidut*), first and foremost, through acts of *hesed*, "lovingkindness."

While Warsaw had a large and vibrant Jewish community, the relationship between Jewish and Christian residents wavered depending on the political and economic situation. Christians often unfairly blamed their Jewish neighbors for local or regional problems, simply because Jews had different religious beliefs and customs and were a smaller, weaker group. Sadly, this was an old pattern throughout Europe that continued to impact the lives of the Jews of Warsaw, including young Heschel and his family. Later in life, he recalled that he had been insulted and roughed up more than once by Christian boys who had already learned to dislike and pick on Jews.

2

MAGICAL ADVENTURES

"Enchanted by a wealth of traditions and tales, I felt truly at home in Mezbizh. That little town so distant from Warsaw and yet so near was the place to which my childish imagination went on many journeys."
—*A Passion for Truth*, 1973

Abraham Joshua enjoyed living in the big, bustling Jewish community of Warsaw, but he also felt a special connection to the much smaller Ukrainian rural settlement of Mezbizh. To an outsider, this quiet country settlement, with its old buildings and surrounding farms, might have looked quaint, but unremarkable. However, his father was born in Mezbizh, and he told his son amazing stories about the residents of his boyhood community.

Mezbizh was home to the first great figure in Hasidic lore, Yisrael ben Eliezer, commonly known as the Ba'al Shem Tov ("Master of the Good Name"). This legendary eighteenth-century man possessed an unusual combination of talents and skills: he was a healer, prayer leader, teacher, and advocate, who helped many people with physical and spiritual challenges. There are countless stories told about the Ba'al Shem Tov; some include reports of magical feats like that of a wizard, sorcerer, or other fabled hero. The title "Master of the Good Name" refers to his ability to use sacred words—including various names for God (the "Good Name" in his title refers to the Divine)—to achieve extraordinary outcomes.

At the heart of the Ba'al Shem Tov's teaching was the conviction that God's loving presence flows through all of creation and that human beings can use this energy to shape meaningful and joyous lives. This approach to Jewish life is sometimes called "mystical," coming from the ancient Greek term for uncovering that which is hidden. The Ba'al Shem Tov was part of a long line of Jewish seekers of this type called *mekubalim*, who received instruction (*kabbalah*) from their teachers and elders on how to undertake the mystical quest.

A key image the Ba'al Shem Tov and his predecessors used to help people experience (*lekabel*) God's presence in their lives was that of light—a spark, a flame, a ray. He encouraged his community members to envision this holy light shining forth from within all of existence, including their own beings. Commenting on the unique influence of this celebrated mystical figure, Heschel wrote that while many Jewish thinkers speak about God, "the Ba'al Shem Tov brought God to the people."

Approximately fifty years after the death of the Ba'al Shem Tov, another great leader came to Mezbizh from the nearby town of Apt (or *Opatow*, in Polish). He was so beloved by his new community that some people thought that the Ba'al Shem Tov had come back to life! This man was none other than the first Avraham Yehoshua Heschel, our Abraham Joshua's great-great-grandfather and namesake. Like the Ba'al Shem Tov, *Zeide* ("Grandfather" or Elder) Heschel also taught people about the need to seek out God's hidden light. He was renowned for his ability to uncover the good in people, including those who were poor or unlearned. The Master from Apt was so well known for his kind ways that he became known as the *Ohev Yisrael*, the Lover of *all* the people of Israel.

One story young Heschel heard directly from his father about the Ohev Yisrael was about their revered Zeide's prayer practice. Many people asked this master to pray on their behalf, believing that God responded more positively to his requests than to those of others, including other Hasidic masters. And so, a group of rebbes visited Mezbizh to learn their colleague's secret of success. The Ohev

Yisrael gently explained to them that he had no magical formulae or special bodily movements, rather, whenever someone came to him with a problem, he tried to relieve them of their suffering by placing some of their pain on his heart. After doing so, he would turn to God in prayer. Seeing the master's wounded heart, the Divine felt compelled to take pity on him and answer his prayers.

3

A HASIDIC PRINCE

"I have one talent and that is the capacity to be tremendously surprised, surprised by life ... This is to me the supreme Hasidic imperative."
—"In Search of Exaltation," 1971

As a child, Abraham Joshua was treated like a prince—a poor prince, but a prince nonetheless—by the members of his Hasidic community. They respected and admired his father and were dedicated to the teachings of the Ba'al Shem Tov, the Ohev Yisrael, and other masters from this distinguished family. The Hasidim showed their esteem for the entire Heschel family, including the littlest member through simple but intentional acts. When, for example, Abraham Joshua entered his father's shteibel, the Hasidim rose from their seats. When he walked through the neighborhood, people greeted him as he passed by, "*Shalom aleikhem* (Peace be upon you), young Heschel!"

Soon, however, Abraham Joshua was recognized because of his own gifts—his own inner light.

Once, while visiting with his close friend Yechiel Hoffer at the Hoffer Family Fabric Store, Abraham Joshua amazed everyone there by quietly memorizing the color, size, style, and price of all the fabrics in the store. "Blue, purple, green; cotton, wool, linen," he could be heard saying, as Yechiel looked on, making sure that his playmate was not peeking. By age six, Abraham Joshua was identified by his teachers as an *illui* (a genius or prodigy). At school, they would raise him on a wooden table and quiz him on various facts about Jewish life. Older students would gather around to hear what he would say next.

This little boy also displayed great sensitivity to human suffering. When Abraham Joshua was just seven years old, he first studied the terrifying story from the Hebrew Bible known as the "Binding of Isaac" (Genesis 22). In this biblical episode, Abraham—the first figure in religious tradition with this name—hears God's voice command him to offer up his beloved son Isaac as a sacrifice.

As the teacher shared the troubling tale with the class, Abraham Joshua sat on the edge of his seat, anxiously waiting to hear the conclusion. "At the last possible instant," said the rabbi, "a heavenly voice called out and saved Isaac and his father from tragedy." At that moment, young Heschel began to cry uncontrollably. The instructor, confused by this reaction, closed his book, and turned to his sad student. "Why are you weeping, child? Don't you understand, Isaac was rescued?" Tears still streaming down his face, Abraham Joshua replied, "But rabbi, suppose the angel had come just a second too late?" Touched by his student's compassion, the teacher put his arm around Abraham Joshua and said to him, "Angels are never late."

Decades later, when Heschel was working as a peace activist, he told this personal story at a large rally but ended it by reminding his audience that while angels are never late, human beings are *often* late—especially when it comes to preventing violence, bloodshed, and warfare.

4

A TIME OF GREAT SADNESS

"Remember that there is meaning beyond absurdity."
—*The Eternal Light* television interview, 1972

In the winter of 1916, a dark shadow fell over the Heschel home. Abraham Joshua's father died just six weeks before his young son's tenth birthday. Rabbi Moshe Mordechai, forty-three years old, was a victim of influenza, a dreadful illness that began sweeping through many countries during an already terrible time: the First World War. Abraham Joshua was heartbroken. As he later told his daughter, he wished that he could have spoken to his father again, "just once more, even for one hour."

With the loss of her husband, Rivka Reizel had to take on even more responsibility. Not only did she care for her children and the home, but she also tended to the shteibel, so that her husband's followers would still have a special place to study and pray. Relatives did all they could to help the Heschels, but it was a very difficult time. Everyone in the family had to help, even Abraham Joshua. He pitched in by going with his big brother Jacob to sell matches and small trinkets in the local outdoor market. Decades later, he recalled that his fingers had become permanently swollen from prolonged exposure to frost during the Warsaw winters.

One person who was particularly supportive of Abraham Joshua during this difficult time was his mother's twin brother, Rabbi Alter Yisrael Shimon Perlow, known in the Hasidic world as the Master from Novominsk (*Minsk Mazowiecki* in Polish). The Novominsker

Rebbe was a kind man, but he was also very strict. He believed that life was a gift from God and not a single moment of it should be wasted. According to family lore, he awoke each morning at sunrise, prayed, studied, and worked all day long, taking only two short breaks for meals: lunch at exactly two o'clock in the afternoon and dinner at midnight.

Rabbi Alter Yisrael Shimon Perlow, The Rebbe from Novominsk (right), with Rabbi Mordechai Shapiro (left) in Warsaw, circa 1929
(Courtesy of Alter Yisrael Shimon Feuerman)

The Novominsker loved Abraham Joshua very much and treated him like a son, even though he had many children of his own. The distinguished rabbi saw great promise in his nephew; he was sure that the boy was going to be an outstanding Hasidic leader. "Someday soon," said the distinguished rabbi, "you will take your rightful place as a rebbe in this holy community." As a sign of respect for his nephew, he asked Abraham Joshua to sit directly next to him on *Shabbos* (Sabbath) afternoons for the third meal, when many

Hasidim and others from the Warsaw Jewish community flocked to the master's home to hear him teach, to sing and eat together, and to savor the last hours of the holy day as a community.

The Novominsker even paid for a private tutor named *Reb* (Mr.) Bezalel Levy to live with his nephew. Like Abraham Joshua's uncle, Reb Bezalel was a very intense and demanding person. He introduced his young mentee to the challenging teachings of the great nineteenth-century master, Rabbi Menachem Mendel of Kotsk. The Kotsker was once asked what it means to be a Hasid. With characteristic sharpness, he said, "To be a Hasid means to work on yourself"—to attempt daily to become a more honest, humble, and responsible person. As Heschel later wrote, while the Ba'al Shem Tov was a source of great comfort, the Rebbe of Kotsk was a source of great challenge. One was like a glowing "lamp," the other like a "lightning" bolt.

Unlike other children his age, Abraham Joshua was not given much time to relax or play. Sometimes, this made him sad. However, he also knew that if he wanted to become a Hasidic master, like the other great men in his family, he would have to work very hard.

5

FINDING LIGHT IN UNEXPECTED PLACES

"God is hiding in the world and our task is to let the Divine emerge from our deeds."
—*God in Search of Man,* 1955

Abraham Joshua continued to develop into a fine master-in-training. He became a *bar mitzvah* (a young Jewish adult, age thirteen), on January 16, 1920. At his bar mitzvah celebration, he delivered the teaching on the weekly Torah portion and had the honor of wearing the *tefillin* (prayer boxes) of one of his renowned ancestors, the eighteenth-century master, Rabbi Levi Yitzhak of Berditchev. By fifteen, he began publishing articles on Jewish law for a journal called *Gates of Torah* (*Sha'arei Torah*). Many people in Hasidic Warsaw assumed that he was on his way to becoming the next great leader in the community. Some people even started to give him *kvitelah* (little notes with their prayers on them), believing that he—like his namesake—had a special connection to God and could help them have their prayers answered. Abraham Joshua was soon ordained as a rabbi based on his mastery of several foundational Jewish legal sources.

But as he grew, Abraham Joshua became increasingly interested in learning a broader range of subjects, including history, mathematics, philosophy, and poetry. While the Polish government required all high schools to provide their students with a basic secular (non-religious) education, the teachers at his *yeshiva* (traditional

Jewish educational institution) discouraged their students from delving too deeply into these areas, viewing them as distractions from the essential task of learning classical Jewish religious literature. These traditional instructors were concerned that their pupils might be tempted away from their sacred way of life by these new ideas.

While limited by what he could study at his yeshiva, Abraham Joshua explored these subjects more in-depth outside of school. He started his adventures somewhat cautiously and did not tell his mother or uncle just how much time he was spending on them. He met some fascinating people at local cafés and other public spaces to discuss contemporary Jewish culture and politics. As one Jewish writer from the area later noted, the local coffeehouse was a place where "people sat…for hours, reading the newspaper, meeting others, talking, sometimes doing everything at once, even those who had just met for the first time." Among those Abraham Joshua encountered in these settings were former Hasidim who were now living more modern lives—some identified as secular, while others continued to practice their religious traditions more selectively. In fact, there were individuals he met with at the local café who also came to his uncle's Shabbos *tisch* (table) on Saturday afternoons for the third meal of the sacred day.

Abraham Joshua proceeded with his secular studies, including improving his knowledge of Polish and learning other languages, including Greek and Latin. He soon found his way to the Yiddish Writers and Journalists Association, which was located just blocks from his Hasidic neighborhood. One of the most prominent members of this professional group was a poet named Melech Ravitch (his pen name), who served as the editor of the Association's literary journal. Ravitch later recalled meeting young Heschel for the first time:

> I raise my eyes and for a moment I am startled. In a corner near my green door stands a…slender young

> lad in Warsaw Hasidic attire. A long black garment almost reaching the ground...a round black hat on his head with a small, pinched, peak.

Though shy and somewhat scared, Abraham Joshua bravely brought Ravitch some of his poems to read, knowing the editor was preparing a new literary collection. Ravitch was impressed with Abraham Joshua's raw ability and creative attempts to bridge the religious and secular worlds between which he was now moving. This included poems on God, poverty, love, and loneliness. The editor published his poetry and prose beginning in 1926 in the journal, *The Literary Pages* (*Literarishe Bleter*).

Several years later, Heschel would publish a collection of Yiddish poetry. In the following poem, he gives powerful voice to a theme that that would become central to his mature writings: the need for human beings to treat one another with dignity and care—including the poor and downtrodden—recognizing the divine essence, or spark, in *all* people (see Genesis 1:26).

God's Tears

God's tears lie on the cheeks
of shamed, weak people.
Let me wipe away God's sorrow.

One in whose veins whirls
a quiet shudder before God
let him kiss the nails of a pauper.
To the worm crushed under-foot
God calls out "My holy martyr!"
The sins of the poor are more beautiful
than the good deeds of the rich.[1]

[1] Translation adapted from Zalman M. Schachter-Shalomi's in *Human—God's Ineffable Name* (Albion-Andalus Books, 2012).

6

FROM WARSAW TO VILNA

"Vilna stood at the center of Eastern European Jewish life.... [It was] the meeting place of poets, philosophers, and religious seekers."

—*A Passion for Truth*, 1973

While Abraham Joshua's mother and uncle were aware of his growing interest in secular education, they were cautious about his path forward. For example, Heschel later recalled that his mother worried when not hearing him chant in Hebrew or Aramaic while studying, knowing he was reading materials other than those of the Jewish sages. It was his family's hope that Abraham Joshua would emerge as a well-informed, contemporary Hasidic master, capable of leading his community at a time when many young people were choosing to leave it.

Discussions with his mother, his uncle, and other trusted relatives intensified when Abraham Joshua told them that he wanted to attend a university, rather than continue his yeshiva studies and begin to serve as a Hasidic rebbe. He explained to his elders that while he still cherished learning traditional Jewish subjects, he wanted to continue to expand his knowledge of the world. To be eligible for admission to a university, Abraham Joshua would first need to spend a year at a modern high school (*gymnasium*) and pass a set of government exams.

After several conversations with his family, Abraham Joshua made the decision to attend a school in Vilna, Lithuania, which was approximately eight hours away from Warsaw by train. While his relatives were very sad to see him go, they understood how determined he was about pursuing his studies. This included saving enough money to pay for his train ticket from his writings for *The Literary Pages*. The Heschel family still hoped that this gifted and impassioned young man would eventually return home to lead his people.

It was on a Saturday night, after the close of the Sabbath, when Abraham Joshua changed his black, velvet Shabbos hat for an ordinary weekday cap and set out on his journey to Vilna. In sending him off into the world, his mother, uncle, and others urged him to remember where he came from, to care for his soul, and to seek out God's hidden light wherever he went.

With that, seventeen-year-old Heschel left for Vilna.

7

THE EMERGENCE OF A POET

"When I wander through boulevards of poetry...
I whisper secrets to that space in which my mysteries reside."
—*Human: God's Ineffable Name*, 1933 (English translation)

Abraham Joshua thrived at the Vilna gymnasium, excelling in his studies, and continuing to write original poetry. While he was somewhat shy and not used to having much time to develop friendships, he was excited to meet peers from different locations and backgrounds—some religious, most not. Together with classmates, he joined a collective for emerging Jewish artists and writers later called Young Vilna. He was impressed with the ways his peers and mentors applied their creativity to real-world problems, including issues of justice for people often abused or neglected by those with greater wealth and power.

While Abraham Joshua no longer dressed like a Hasid or studied only religious sources, he remained observant of Jewish sacred practices, including reciting daily prayers, keeping a kosher (traditional Jewish) diet, and celebrating the Sabbath and holidays—and proud of his family's heritage. He rented a small room in a house owned by an older religious man in a poor neighborhood. He also traveled home to Warsaw, when possible, to visit his family.

One way in which Abraham Joshua maintained a distinctive Hasidic perspective was in his understanding of the spiritual significance of the natural world. One of his classmates in Vilna, Shlomo

Beilis, recalled taking a walk together that led them to a forest just outside the city. Beilis, who came from a secular background, was moved by Heschel's description of the woods as a "holy place" (*makom kadosh* in Hebrew) in which one can cultivate a sense of reverence for God's creation. This statement echoes the words of the biblical poet who centuries earlier wrote, "How wonderous are your works Eternal One, how profound your designs" (Psalm 92:6, the Sabbath Psalm).

Book cover of Heschel's first publication, *Human: God's Ineffable Name*, translation by Rabbi Zalman M. Schachter-Shalomi
(Courtesy of Netanel Miles-Yépez, Albion-Andalus Books)

Later in life, Heschel would write at greater length about this sensibility, describing it as "radical amazement." In coining this term, he attempted to awaken people to the remarkable fact that there are "facts at all." Once, when giving a lecture at a prominent synagogue in London, England, he opened with the following statement:

"An hour ago there took place the greatest event in all history." The audience sat up in surprise. "The sunset!" Heschel stated. His host that evening, Rabbi Dr. Louis Jacobs, remarked, "That was enough to remind even this staid [serious and formal] English gathering that our seemingly ordinary existence is shot through with wonder."

8

SCHOLARSHIP AND SPIRITUALITY

"As civilization advances, the sense of wonder declines. Mankind will not perish for want of information, but only for want of appreciation.... Life without wonder is not worth living."
—*God in Search of Man*, 1955

After graduating from high school in 1927, Heschel traveled from Vilna to Berlin, Germany to begin his university studies. At the time, Berlin was the great center of modern life in Europe. There were many museums, concert halls, theaters, and sporting events. Berlin also had excellent schools for Jewish studies. Now a twenty-year-old man, Heschel was excited to begin his adult life in such a dazzling city. Still, he was very poor and struggled to pay for his basic needs; this worsened with onset of the Great Depression beginning in late 1929. During this time of widespread poverty, untold numbers of people struggled with food, clothing, and housing. There were times when the only things he had to eat were bread and potatoes.

Heschel enrolled in the Royal Friedrich Wilhelm University (now Humboldt University) of Berlin, where he studied philosophy, art history, and ancient Hebrew and other regional languages. He also continued to learn a wide range of Jewish subjects at two outstanding Jewish institutions: The Academy for the Scientific Study of Judaism—more liberal—and The Rabbinical Seminary for

Orthodox Judaism—more traditional. A key element to his development in these years was his willingness to open himself to the ideas and opinions of different talented scholars, teachers, and classmates, while forging his own authentic way in the world. This was a challenge for the emerging scholar and writer, who was moving daily between different religious and cultural communities. It sometimes left him feeling lonely.

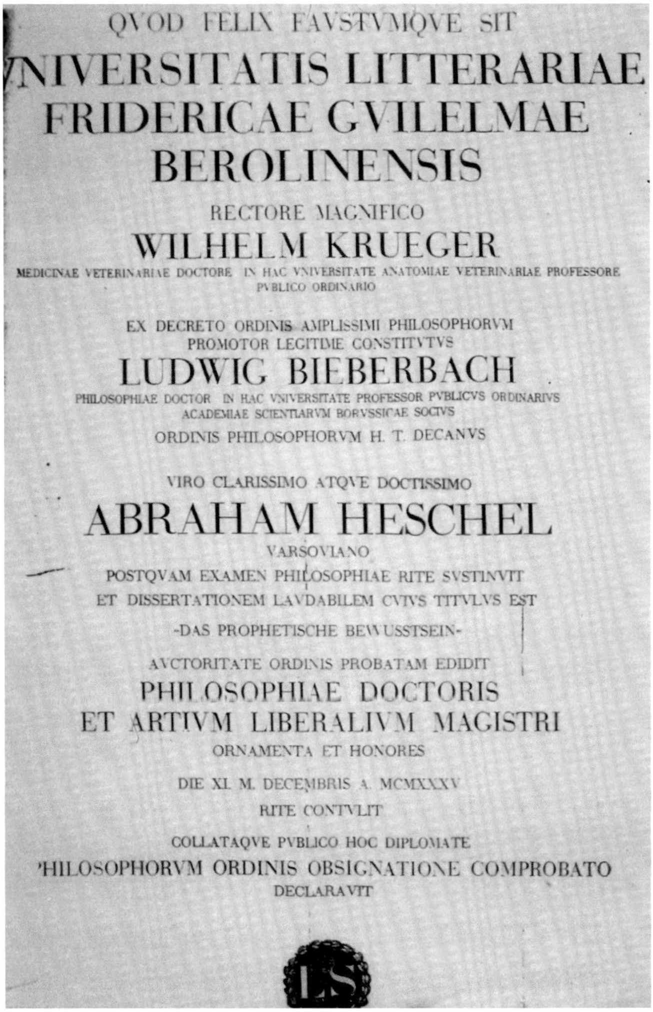

QVOD FELIX FAVSTVMQVE SIT
VNIVERSITATIS LITTERARIAE
FRIDERICAE GVILELMAE
BEROLINENSIS
RECTORE MAGNIFICO
WILHELM KRUEGER
MEDICINAE VETERINARIAE DOCTORE IN HAC VNIVERSITATE ANATOMIAE VETERINARIAE PROFESSORE PVBLICO ORDINARIO

EX DECRETO ORDINIS AMPLISSIMI PHILOSOPHORVM
PROMOTOR LEGITIME CONSTITVTVS
LUDWIG BIEBERBACH
PHILOSOPHIAE DOCTOR IN HAC VNIVERSITATE PROFESSOR PVBLICVS ORDINARIVS
ACADEMIAE SCIENTIARVM BORVSSICAE SOCIVS
ORDINIS PHILOSOPHORVM H. T. DECANVS

VIRO CLARISSIMO ATQVE DOCTISSIMO
ABRAHAM HESCHEL
VARSOVIANO
POSTQVAM EXAMEN PHILOSOPHIAE RITE SVSTINVIT
ET DISSERTATIONEM LAVDABILEM CVIVS TITVLVS EST
-DAS PROPHETISCHE BEWUSSTSEIN-
AVCTORITATE ORDINIS PROBATAM EDIDIT
PHILOSOPHIAE DOCTORIS
ET ARTIVM LIBERALIVM MAGISTRI
ORNAMENTA ET HONORES
DIE XI. M. DECEMBRIS A. MCMXXXV
RITE CONTVLIT
COLLATAQVE PVBLICO HOC DIPLOMATE
PHILOSOPHORVM ORDINIS OBSIGNATIONE COMPROBATO
DECLARAVIT

Heschel's PhD diploma
(Courtesy of Edward K. Kaplan)

For example, in an essay he wrote decades later about Jewish ritual and law, Heschel recalled once taking a leisurely walk home after completing a long day of classes and meetings at the university. As the sun set over the magnificent streets of Berlin, he thought about the intense discussions he had with his professors and classmates about the history of religious ideas, texts, and rituals. While he found these explorations vital to his growth as a scholar, they did not nourish his soul. As a religious person, he did not want to only talk about spiritual matters, but to cultivate a relationship with God and actively engage in Jewish sacred practice. With that, he gazed into the night sky and began chanting the words of the *Ma'ariv* (Evening) prayer service:

> Blessed are you, God,
> King of the Universe,
> Who by your word brings on the evening twilight.

9

THE FLAMES OF THE HOLOCAUST

"Human life is holy, holier even than the scrolls of the Torah."
—"Symbolism and the Jewish Faith," 1954

Tragically, Heschel was living in Berlin during a time in history when many Germans were unable or unwilling to recognize the sacredness in all people. Adolf Hitler (1889-1945), leader of the Nazi political party and a vicious antisemite (hater of Jews), was named Chancellor of Germany on January 30, 1933. He claimed that Jews and other minorities (including people of color, people with disabilities, and homosexuals) were responsible for all the problems in the country. Hitler said that life would be much better if only these undesirable people were removed from society.

Far too many Germans believed Hitler's twisted lies, and his spirit of hatred spread like wildfire.

Increasingly, the Nazis and their followers instituted discriminatory policies that pushed Jews to the margins of German society. When, for example, Heschel first arrived at the university, he had Jewish professors, but they were soon forced out of their positions and replaced by Christian professors, supportive of Hitler's antisemitic agenda.

Ironically, Heschel's doctoral thesis (major research project) was a study of the prophets of the Hebrew Bible, who in their time and place raged against the mistreatment of people, especially those with less power and influence. But now, he and his fellow Jews were being abused by the Nazis and their followers. While Heschel submitted his thesis in December 1932, he only received his PhD (from the Latin for "Doctorate in Philosophy") in December 1935. The reason for this unusually long wait was that after Hitler came to power it became increasingly difficult for Jewish authors to publish their writing in Germany, and doctoral students had to publish their work to receive their diplomas.

Once, when Heschel attended a concert, Adolf Hitler entered the hall. The budding Jewish scholar was horrified when he saw the audience stand in honor of this dreadful man. Heschel quietly walked out as soon as possible. He was astounded that Germany—the great center of modern civilization—was spellbound by this hateful and manipulative person. Clearly, there was a widening gap between the cultural and moral sensibilities of this nation. Heschel hoped and prayed that the German public would quickly come to its senses and abandon its support of the Nazis.

While finishing his university studies, Heschel also completed rabbinic training at the Academy for the Scientific Study of Judaism (having already received traditional ordination as a teenager in Warsaw) and began teaching there and in the broader German Jewish community. He also wrote poetry, articles, and books, seeking to educate and inspire readers, including those unfamiliar with classical Jewish thought, at a time when their heritage and humanity were increasingly under attack. He urged his community to proudly invest in their religious and cultural traditions as acts of spiritual resistance against this new wave of Jew-hatred.

In the spring of 1933, the Nazis organized a massive public burning of Jewish and other books they considered "un-German." In response, Heschel published a long Yiddish poem entitled "On the Day of Hate." Writing under the penname "Itsik" ("Isaac") to protect himself from Nazi backlash, he described how the city of Berlin looked like a "volcano" as thousands of Jewish works were removed from libraries and thrown into a huge public bonfire. In sharp contrast to this horrible display of inhumanity, that same year

Heschel, now twenty-six years old, published his first book, a collection of sixty-six Yiddish poems—including pieces written during his years in Warsaw and Vilna. The title of the volume is *God's Ineffable* (Unspeakable) *Name: The Human Being* (*Der Shem ha'Meforash: Mentsch*). The title includes a reference to the ancient Hebrew name for God—*Y-H-W-H*—which is considered the most sacred term for the Divine in the Jewish tradition. According to an age-old teaching, this mysterious name—which has no consonants—was pronounced only once a year, on the holiest of days—*Yom Kippur* (the Day of Atonement)—by the high priest in the innermost chamber of the Temple in Jerusalem. Otherwise, it remained unspoken. To this day, religious Jews avoid trying to pronounce or write it. Heschel was reminding his readers of the holiness of the human being; urging them to treat every single person as a unique and mysterious expression of God's love and creativity. Heschel dedicated the volume to his late father, Rabbi Moshe Mordechai, his first teacher of dignity and compassion.

From 1933 to 1945, antisemitism was the official law of the land in Germany and the other countries it conquered during World War II. Millions of Jews were forced from their homes and made to live in cramped, unhealthy places called ghettos, or carted off to miserable concentration camps where they were tortured and murdered. The most intense period—1941-45—of this horrific campaign is known as the *Holocaust* (Greek for "burnt offering") or the *Shoah* (Hebrew for "catastrophe"). By the end of the war, the Nazis and their collaborators had murdered six million Jews, approximately one-third of the global Jewish population at the time. The Nazis killed several million more non-Jewish people whom they considered enemies or simply undeserving of life.

The violent flames of the Holocaust were the exact *opposite* of the holy light the Ba'al Shem Tov had spoken of so long ago.

10

FORCED RETURN, NARROW ESCAPE

"I am a brand plucked from the fire on which my people was burned."
—"No Religion Is an Island," 1965

In January 1937, just a few days after celebrating his thirtieth birthday, Heschel moved from Berlin, the capital city of Germany, to Frankfurt. He went there to become a teacher at the Center for Adult Jewish Education, which was established by Dr. Martin Buber, one of the most prominent Jewish intellectuals in Europe. Soon, however, Dr. Buber took leave for Palestine as Nazism continued to spread throughout the country. Heschel, too, wanted to flee Germany, but as a younger professional he had limited options. So he took on the responsibility of co-directing the Center after Buber's departure and continued to teach and write on a range of Jewish topics. Heschel attempted to support and inspire his community during a time of mounting pain and fear, while anxiously looking for work elsewhere in Europe and beyond.

Heschel's time in Germany ended very suddenly late on a cold autumn night in 1938. He was awoken from his sleep by a loud knock at the door. "Abraham Heschel, this is the police. Open the door immediately." The officers went on to inform him that Jewish people from Poland were being expelled from Germany. He was given one hour to pack two bags. Alone and frightened, Heschel quickly gathered up his essential belongings and carried his suitcases to the Frankfurt police headquarters under the watchful eye of Nazi policemen. He was held overnight in a tiny prison cell, and the next day he was shoved onto an overcrowded train with thousands of other Polish Jews. The trip home was terrible: It took three long days and Heschel had to stand for most of the ride. This was certainly not how he wanted to leave the country or return to his birthplace.

Abraham Joshua Heschel in Frankfurt, Germany (1938), where he relocated to teach at the Center for Adult Jewish Education
(Photograph by Atelier May; Courtesy of Edward K. Kaplan)

When the train finally arrived at the Polish border, the local officials refused to admit the Jews. Hitler's influence had already spread to Poland. Heschel and the others were held at the border in inhumane conditions. Many people remained there for months. Heschel was very fortunate as his family was able to arrange for his release after just a few days. He spent the next ten months teaching at the Warsaw Institute of Jewish Study. While reunited with his mother and other family members, it was a time of great distress for them knowing that the Nazis were on the warpath.

In the spring of 1939, Heschel received a lifeline in the form of an invitation to join the faculty of Hebrew Union College (HUC), a Reform (the major liberal denomination) Jewish university in far-off Cincinnati, Ohio. Rabbi Dr. Julian Morgenstern, the president of the school, was working tirelessly to save Jewish scholars from the Nazis. Heschel responded to the invitation by thanking Dr. Morgenstern for his leadership during "this sorrowful time." However, Heschel was deeply pained because he could not take his family with him. It was his hope that once he arrived safely in America, he could speak to other caring people who might help his family escape from the Nazis.

In the summer of 1939, Heschel left Warsaw for London, England, as he waited nervously for the United States government to approve his immigration papers. There, he was reunited with his older brother, Rabbi Jacob Heshel (he spelled his name in English without the letter "c"), who had recently escaped the Nazis with his wife and children, serving as the spiritual leader of an Orthodox synagogue. While in London, Abraham Joshua also helped establish a center for adult Jewish education similar to the one in Frankfurt. Tragically, just six weeks after he left Poland, the Germans invaded, crushed the city of Warsaw, and began brutalizing its Jewish community. The Heschel family suffered greatly: Esther Sima was killed in the initial bombing, and Rivka Reizel and Gittel fled the family apartment to avoid serious injury but would later be murdered by the Nazis (as would Devorah Miriam).

Abraham Joshua Heschel would never return to Poland or Germany. He stated that if he should return to either country, "every stone, every tree," would remind him of "hatred" and "murder."

11

SAFETY AND SORROW IN AMERICA

"There is an evil which most of us condone and are even guilty of: indifference to evil. We remain neutral, impartial, and not easily moved by the wrongs done to other people."
—"Religion and Race," 1963

After months of waiting, Heschel's visa was approved and he set sail for the United States, arriving in New York City on March 21, 1940. He spent the first few months living with his oldest sister, Sarah, her husband, the Kapitshinitzer Rebbe (Kopychyntsi, Ukraine), and their children on the Lower East Side of Manhattan. The Heschel siblings were very thankful to be reunited. Not only were they both living in a new country (Sarah and her family arrived in 1939), but they constantly worried about the safety and well-being of their family members in Europe.

In the fall of 1940, Heschel began teaching at HUC in Cincinnati.

While he was forever grateful to the school for saving his life, the five years he spent there were very difficult. He was alone in a new part of the world and one of the only people at the college who lived a traditional Jewish lifestyle. He could not eat most of the food in the school's dining hall because it was not kosher. Faculty and students were surprised by Heschel's attachment to the "old ways" and he by their disinterest in these classical forms of practice. But Heschel did develop close relationships with some colleagues and students at HUC, including a group of young men who were light-heartedly called the "Kavannah Boys" by their peers, because they were attracted to Heschel's message of the beauty of the Sabbath and other classical observances as ways to develop intentional (*kavannah*) and intensive relationships with God, with other people, and with the natural world.

Heschel (second to left) sitting with Rabbi Dr. Julian Morgenstern (center right) and the other Jewish scholars saved from the Holocaust by Hebrew Union College, Cincinnati, Ohio, circa 1942
(Courtesy of the American Jewish Archives)

Heschel's greatest challenge during this time was, of course, trying to save his family and friends from the Nazis. He spoke to American leaders about the viciousness of the Nazis; he made public speeches at synagogues and Jewish community centers, and even sent what little money he had back to his relatives in Poland. Despite his efforts, his three sisters perished at the hands of the Nazis, and Heschel's mother, Rivka Reizel, suffered a deadly heart attack when German soldiers appeared at her apartment door. Within just five years, Heschel mourned the loss of four immediate family members.

Heartbreakingly, Heschel learned all of this while he was alone in Cincinnati. He arranged various communal prayer services (*minyanim*) at the HUC campus, so that he could recite the mourner's *Kaddish* ("Sanctification," prayer for the dead) for his loved ones with the support of others.

Among the people in Cincinnati whom Heschel befriended was Rabbi Eliezer Silver, an Orthodox (the major traditional denomination) rabbi originally from Eastern Europe. On October 6, 1943—between the Jewish observance of *Rosh Hashanah* (New Year) and Yom Kippur—Rabbi Silver led a rally of four hundred rabbis in Washington, DC, to protest the Nazi slaughter of European Jewry. Heschel participated in this march, hoping it would move President Franklin Delano Roosevelt and his administration to take strong action on behalf of European Jewry. Tragically, the President did not heed the call of the rabbinic protestors, as he had heard from advisors, including some prominent American Jewish leaders, that these marchers were misinformed and the situation in Europe was not nearly as bad as they claimed.

While this rally was unsuccessful, it did plant important seeds in Heschel's mind on the role of such protests in the pursuit of justice.

A related question that gripped Heschel in these years—and for the rest of his life—was what God's role during this horrific period in human history. If the Creator was loving and powerful, why allow the Nazis to perpetrate such unthinkable crimes? Did God not care? Was the Divine unable to stop these despicable acts? Were the Jewish people and other victims of the Nazi onslaught somehow deserving of severe punishment?

Heschel believed that human beings, not God, were responsible for the Holocaust. He argued that the Creator gives us free will—the ability to choose how to think and behave. While God is often deeply pained and disappointed by the choices people make, the Divine respects humankind too much to take away our freedom. And so, in the case of the Shoah, God wept bitterly as the Nazis and their collaborators carried out their reign of terror, and far too many others—in Europe, North America, and elsewhere—did not act to stop this monstrous campaign. As Heschel stated emphatically on different occasions, “The question is *not* where was God in Auschwitz [the largest of the Nazi concentration camps], but where was man?”

12

LOVE, MARRIAGE, AND FAMILY

"How much I wish to be in love, to be close to someone.... Come and take my heart's dearest treasure, my love."
—*Human: God's Ineffable Name*, 1933 (English translation)

In 1945, as the war in Europe was finally ending, Heschel was offered a teaching position at the Jewish Theological Seminary (JTS) in New York City. The center for Conservative Judaism, this school was a better fit for him religiously, as its leaders were more traditional practitioners, but also valued the modern study of Torah and other sacred sources. New York City was also one of the great Jewish and American cultural centers, offering Heschel many new opportunities to mingle with scholars, religious leaders, writers, and artists from all over the world.

It was in New York that Heschel rekindled a romantic relationship with a Jewish woman he had first dated in Cincinnati. Sylvia Straus was a concert pianist and the daughter of Jewish refugees from Eastern Europe. She had a love of the arts and a commitment to Jewish religious life.

Abraham and Sylvia Heschel married on December 10, 1946, in Los Angeles, where her parents resided. He was thirty-nine years old and she was thirty-three. After six lonely years in America, with just a few close relatives and friends, now Heschel had someone with whom he could share his life, in good times and bad. The Heschels moved to an apartment at 425 Riverside Drive on the Upper West Side of Manhattan, just blocks away from his new workplace. They were also able to spend time with other relatives in the New York area, including Heschel's sister, Sarah, and her family.

On May 15, 1952, the couple had a baby girl, their only child, whom they named Channa Shoshanah—Susannah is her English name. Heschel adored his daughter and loved to play games with her like "red light, green light" and "schoolhouse." As a child, he had virtually no time for such things because of his studies, but now as a father he took the time to play with his daughter.

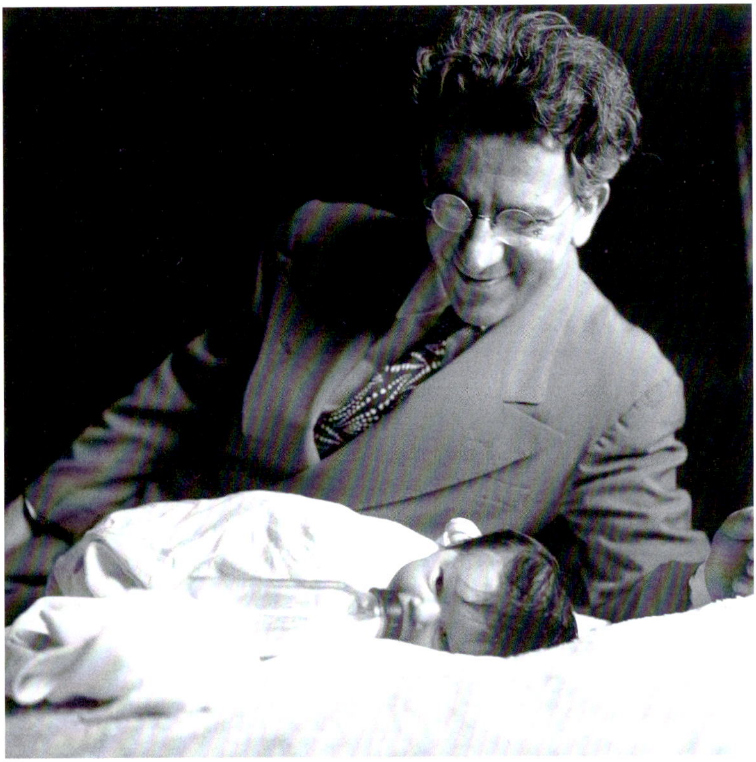

Heschel with his newborn baby, Susannah, 1952
(Photograph by Lotte Jacobi; Courtesy of the Lotte Jacobi Collection, University of New Hampshire)

As an adult, Susannah wrote the following about life with her father:

> I remember as a child walking with my father along Broadway, in dirty, noisy, grimy streets, and then

> turning the corner to go home, walking down the hill toward Riverside Drive, and seeing before us the Hudson River and, sometimes, a magnificent sunset. My father would describe what we were seeing, the wonder of God's miracles in nature, the beauty of a sunset that reminds us of God's presence in the world.

When she grew up, Susannah became a professor and chair of the Jewish studies program at Dartmouth College. Professor Susannah Heschel is the author and editor of many books and articles on Judaism and Christianity, and the recipient of various awards and honors. She has also been an outspoken advocate for justice—like her father—especially for women. In 1995, she married Dr. James Aronson, professor of geology at Dartmouth College. They have two adult daughters: Avigael Natania Mira, named for her grandfathers (and a cousin), and Gittel Esther Devorah, named for Abraham Joshua Heschel's three sisters murdered in the Holocaust.

13

RELIGIOUS SPEAKER AND WRITER

"Religion consists of God's question and man's answer."
—*God in Search of Man*, 1955

Within a few years after his arrival to the United States, Heschel began to publish widely in English—a language he only began learning as an adult in Germany. His first English book (1949) was based on a speech he gave in New York City in 1946 for YIVO (the Yiddish acronym for the Institute for Jewish Research, originally located in Vilna), a leading center for the study of Eastern European Jewish culture and history.

In his address, he spoke lovingly and longingly about religious life in this once thriving civilization. Heschel addressed his audience in Yiddish—his *mamme loshen* ("mother tongue")—and the language of daily Jewish life in his birthplace. He inspired his listeners with stories about great masters and sages, but also about their communities. His audience, largely secular, was so moved by his words that when he finished, they stood and recited the Kaddish together for all the victims of the Shoah.

When Heschel published this speech as a book, *The Earth Is the Lord's: The Inner World of the Jew in Eastern Europe*, he signed it using his full name, Abraham Joshua Heschel—the name he was called as a boy in Poland.

In the 1950s, Abraham Joshua Heschel established himself as a highly respected religious voice in his new homeland. He wrote many inspiring books and taught Jews and non-Jews throughout the world about the need for people to treat one another, and all other living beings, with care and compassion. A book reviewer from *Time* magazine was so impressed with one of Heschel's books that he said it "sings and soars" like the teachings of "the great . . . Hasidic leaders from whom he is descended." The Reverend Dr. Reinhold Niebuhr, one of America's most influential Christian public intellectuals, and someone who became a close friend to Heschel, expressed his surprise that this recent immigrant from European could write so beautifully on such complex matters in English. Dr. Niebuhr celebrated Heschel as a new "commanding voice" in American public life. One of Heschel's true gifts was his ability to use language to open people's hearts *and* minds. He did so in several different languages.

Heschel speaking at The Jewish Theological Seminary in 1946
(Courtesy of The Jewish Theological Seminary)

In one of Heschel's major works, *God in Search of Man: A Philosophy of Judaism* (1955), he wrote at length about "radical amazement," arguing that every person is born with a sense of wonder. This, he insisted, is something we can access throughout our lives when seeing a sunset, smelling flowers, or tasting a piece of fruit. He added that such experiences are God's way of lovingly calling us to serve as partners in fostering a world of compassion and justice. What does it mean to be a "religious" person, Heschel asked? To understand that "love" is our greatest "strength."

While many spiritual teachers have written about the human search for God, Heschel insisted that God is forever searching for *us*; inviting every single human being to use their unique gifts and abilities to improve the world. Heschel claimed that the Hebrew Bible can be summarized in one phrase: "God is in search of man." The challenge, he said, was to pay attention to the signs (or sparks of light) and then to develop the discipline to be our best selves.

Heschel encouraged people to view the human face as an immediate and concrete sign of God's loving presence in our lives. Each of us is a unique representation of the Divine—the invisible Creator of all faces. This is why no two faces are alike. Even identical twins are not quite identical! Furthermore, no single face remains the same "for more than an instant." Heschel insisted that only by developing our capacity for lovingkindness—for God, for humankind, and for creation—could the world avoid the horrors of the recent past. Philosophy, science, and the arts are all very valuable, but they are not enough; we need "pathos" (compassion or mercy, Greek origin) or *hesed*.

Throughout his teachings, Heschel spoke at length about the special role that prayer can play in our attempts to answer God's call. He explained that the primary purpose of prayer is to express our appreciation for the gifts in our lives. It is also a time to consider how to use these gifts for the greater good. Heschel viewed the traditional Jewish requirement to pray regularly as training for a life of gratitude and responsibility. As he wrote, "The words of prayer are commitments. We stand for what we utter.... [Our prayer] is like a pledge in the making." He continued by reminding readers that prayer is not a "substitute for action," but rather like a "beam" of light with which we can explore our values and priorities, so that we can take purposeful action in the world.

Another of Heschel's influential works is a slim volume called *The Sabbath: Its Meaning for Modern Man* (1951). In this book, he describes how God created the seventh day of the week as a special time for celebration and renewal. Using his skill as a poet, he called Shabbos a "palace in time." As with a physical palace, the Sabbath is a distinctive and beautiful "dwelling" in which, like royalty, we can enjoy the riches of family, friends, and nature.

Heschel argued that the Sabbath is of particular importance in the modern era because of the fast pace at which people live and work. He explained that on Shabbos we are invited to temporarily "turn away" from inventing, building, and overcoming, and simply enjoy and give thanks for the gifts of life. This, he argued, could help us—like prayer—develop greater appreciation for all that is given to us by the Creator, and inspire us to return to the work of serving humbly and humanely as God's partners during the other six days of the week.

> To set apart one day a week for freedom . . . a day for being with ourselves, a day of detachment . . . of independence of external obligations.... Is there any institution that holds out greater hope for man's progress than the Sabbath?

In making his argument, Heschel said that we must recover an appreciation of the holiness of *time*, instead of constantly trying to master the realm of *space*. After all, human beings have but limited time on this earth; we should, therefore, seek to live purposefully and joyously. Building large buildings or grand monuments cannot extend our lives nor make them more meaningful. In the opening pages of *The Sabbath*, he reminds readers that the first time the word *kadosh* ("holy") appears in the Hebrew Bible, it references the Seventh Day (Genesis 2:3). God designates this time as sacred before any object or place.

Heschel in his office at the Jewish Theological Seminary (1960), where he taught for much of his career in the United States
(Courtesy of The Jewish Theological Seminary)

14

TEACHER AND MENTOR

"What we need more than anything else is not textbooks *but* textpeople.
It is the personality of the teacher which is the text that the pupils read;
the text that they will never forget."
—*The Insecurity of Freedom*, 1955

At JTS, Heschel divided his time between research and writing and teaching and mentoring young adults. Most of his students were preparing for careers as Jewish communal professionals—rabbis, cantors, and teachers. Although he was often called away to participate in pressing religious and political matters, he attempted to bring insights from the wider world back to the classroom. On occasion, he would begin a class session by sharing with students a letter he had received from an organization or individual seeking his advice.

One such letter came from the president of a small synagogue in the Bronx, New York. The individual writing explained to Heschel that the synagogue board had decided to close their doors because most of the members had moved to a new housing development in a different neighborhood. And so, the synagogue leadership decided to sell the building and use the proceeds to reopen in the new location. In the meantime, they had two potential buyers of their existing space, each offering an equal amount of money: a Baptist church and a bank. "To whom do you think we should sell the building?" asked the synagogue president.

After reading the letter to his class of rabbinical students, Heschel stroked his beard and asked: "So, gentlemen, you are all soon to become rabbis [there were no women yet in the JTS rabbinical school], what is your *p'sak*, what is your Jewish legal decision?"

Following a few moments of uncomfortable silence, one student at the back of the room raised his hand and stated confidently, "I recently read a classic medieval work on Jewish law and the author stated that one is not to sell a synagogue to a church because of fundamental difference of belief between Judaism and Christianity. Therefore, my answer is that the people in the Bronx must sell their building to the bank."

Heschel listened carefully to his eager student, smiled, and said: "Forgive me, but I must disagree. They may *not* sell the synagogue to the bank. If it is sold to the Baptists, it will remain a temple of *God*; if it is sold to the bank, it will become a temple of *money*. And we already have more than enough of these temples."[1]

Heschel particularly enjoyed teaching and mentoring small groups or individual students whom he could get to know more personally. This included Jewish and non-Jewish individuals. Among his closest younger associates (by twenty years or so) was the Reverend William Sloane Coffin, Jr., a gifted Christian (Protestant) speaker, writer, and social activist. The two men met through their peace work in the mid-1960s. Rev. Coffin respected and admired his Jewish mentor and colleague, affectionately referring to Heschel as "Father" Abraham—a title usually reserved for priests.

In his memoir, Coffin recalls how shortly after meeting Heschel, the Rabbi invited him to Shabbos dinner at their family home on Riverside Drive. The Reverend goes on to describe how delightful it was for him to participate in the special Friday night meal—including blessings and song—with Heschel, his wife Sylvia, and their

---

[1] My father, Rabbi Dr. Neal Rose, was a student in the class and shared this story with me. —Or N. Rose

teenage daughter Susannah. Coffin and his host talked until one in the morning, moving between lighthearted banter and more serious discussion of religion and contemporary life. The Reverend left feeling very grateful to have made this new interreligious friendship. With characteristic wit and warmth, he ends his reflection by stating, "I couldn't see why any Christian would want Heschel to accept Jesus Christ as his Lord and Savior." Like his Jewish friend and mentor, Coffin believed that the one God of all humankind desires religious pluralism, that people express their commitments in different ways based on their authentic beliefs and values, and treat one another with dignity and care.

In his role as informal teacher and guide, Heschel followed in the footsteps of the Hasidic masters and other mentors he met along his unusual path to America. Although he did not return to his childhood community to serve as a traditional rebbe, he served as a spiritual advisor to students and colleagues from different walks of life.

Heschel and Rev. William Sloane Coffin Jr., 1969
(Photograph by John C. Goodwin; Courtesy of Edward K. Kaplan)

Heschel's twenty-five years at JTS were rewarding, but also challenging. While he was more aligned with his New York colleagues than those in Cincinnati in terms of Jewish observance, other differences created painful distance. Heschel was an unconventional scholar and writer. He wrote several books for broad audiences, while other prominent JTS scholars wrote for fellow experts. He also focused much of his writing on theology—the study of the relationship between God, humankind, and the world (Greek for *Theos*, "God" and *logos*, "speech")—while his seminary peers largely concentrated on Jewish history, languages, and law.

Heschel's Hasidic background and passion for Jewish mystical teachings also set him apart from several of the other JTS faculty, who were raised in Jewish communities in Eastern and Central Europe that existed in tension with Hasidism. Finally, as Heschel became increasingly involved in social justice issues in the last decade of his life, he received significant public attention. His strong stances and growing media presence drew a range of responses from his peers, including agreement, support, and pride, but also disagreement, opposition, and jealousy. For all the above reasons, Heschel found himself at odds with various colleagues, including some institutional leaders. These rifts were painful to him personally and also limited his leadership opportunities within the institution.

15

IN THE FOOTSTEPS OF THE PROPHETS

"Life is clay, and righteousness the mold in which God wants history to be shaped."
—"Religion and Race," 1963

It was in the early 1960s, while finishing an expanded English version of his doctoral thesis on the prophets of the Hebrew Bible—the ancient champions of compassion and justice—that Heschel began to dedicate more time and energy to contemporary societal issues. He later stated that even though he felt most comfortable in his study, where he could quietly read and write, the prophets taught him that he had to become more involved in "the affairs of suffering man."

Of course, his agonizing experiences as a refugee from Nazi-occupied Europe also informed his sense of responsibility. Heschel dedicated *The Prophets* (1962) to all the victims of the Holocaust, and his major Hebrew work on rabbinic interpretations of the Hebrew Bible, *Torah min ha'Shamayim* ("Heavenly Torah," 1962, volume one of three), to his mother and three sisters. The latter opens as follows:

> In memory of my mother, the righteous (*tzaddeket*)
> Rivka Reizel,
> and in memory of my sisters:
> Devora Miriam, Esther Sima, and Gittel

who perished in the Shoah.
May their souls be bound up in the bond of life.

One of the issues Heschel took up was the plight of Jews in the Soviet Union. He spoke out against the Soviet government because it was not allowing Jews to practice their religion or culture freely; they could be arrested simply for speaking Hebrew. Heschel reminded the American public that just as African Americans were fighting for liberty in the United States, so too were Jews in Russia and other parts of the Soviet Union. The only difference was that people in America were either unaware of or not yet willing to help their Jewish brothers and sisters in this far-away land. Heschel insisted that his fellow Americans participate in both causes, as "the evil of prejudice is indivisible."

Among the people with whom he worked on this cause was his friend Elie Wiesel, whose writings, including the autobiographical *Night* (1958), helped millions of readers throughout the world understand the true horrors of the Holocaust and the need for personal and collective action in the face of evil. Many North American Jews soon took up the plight of Soviet Jewry and began protesting in front of Soviet government buildings, writing letters to their senators and congressmen, and contacting and visiting Jews in different Soviet cities and towns, urging them not to lose hope. One newspaper, the *New York Daily News*, published a photograph of Heschel holding a placard at a demonstration that read, "Jews Demand Equal Rights in the Soviet Union." This movement eventually led to the improvement of countless numbers of Jewish lives, including those who remained in their homeland and those who emigrated to the United States, Israel, and elsewhere.

Heschel was also involved in public efforts to foster greater respect and cooperation among people from different religions. Between 1962 and 1965, he served as an unofficial advisor to a historic set of meetings the Roman Catholic Church organized called The Second Vatican Council (the first such meeting took place ninety years earlier). Among the key issues Church leaders discussed was the relationship between Catholicism to Judaism and Catholics to Jews. The two groups had been locked in an antagonistic relationship for thousands of years. As the more powerful partner in the relationship, Catholic leaders and their communities inflicted great pain on Jews throughout the centuries, including limiting their rights and subjecting them to physical violence. They justified these abusive actions through religious instruction about the sinful beliefs and practices of Jews. The gravest of these teachings was the false claim that the Jewish people was responsible for the murder of Jesus of Nazareth, whom Christians classically regard as the earthly embodiment of God (or "Son of God"). The horrific claim of *deicide* ("killing God" in Latin) was used repeatedly to depict Jews as a blood-thirsty and cursed nation.

While Hitler's demonic campaign was not carried out in the name of Christianity, centuries of Christian hatred and cruelty towards Jews—including during Heschel's early years in Warsaw—made it much easier for the Nazis to convince people that Jews were evil and should be treated as such. Further, Christian leaders—Catholic, Protestant, and others—did not do nearly enough to oppose the Nazis and save Jews from torment and death. Far too few Christian clergy demonstrated the kind of moral courage one would expect of religious leaders in such a crisis.

Heschel found his conversations with Pope Paul VI, Cardinal Augustine Bea (a fellow scholar of the Hebrew Bible), and other Catholic leaders both promising and painful. He felt that history demanded dramatic change, including the Church putting an end to its persistent efforts to convert Jews to Christianity over many centuries.

There were times when he became frustrated and impatient with the long, drawn-out, and bureaucratic process at Vatican II. The more than 2,000 Catholic delegates from around the world had significant internal differences in belief and strategy, debating the issues for three years. Adding to the complexity of the situation, some prominent rabbis criticized Heschel and the other Jewish delegates for negotiating with Catholic counterparts over issues that the Church should have addressed centuries earlier. In the end, Heschel considered his efforts a partial success. The official document, *Nostra Aetate* ("In Our Time," Latin), decried all "displays of anti-Semitism" and called for "mutual understanding and respect" between Christians and Jews. However, it did not mention the issue of conversion explicitly, and was ambiguous in its statement about the responsibility of Jewish people for the murder of Jesus Christ ("Anointed One," Messiah), declaring that this charge cannot be made against "all the Jews."

Still, Heschel felt that there were many noble Catholics involved in the Second Vatican Council and that the three-year process represented a major step forward in healing relations between the Jewish and Christian communities.

Over the next several years, Heschel participated in other significant interreligious initiatives. For example, in 1965 he was invited to serve as the first visiting Jewish professor at Union Theological Seminary, an esteemed Protestant institution located across the street from JTS in Manhattan. Heschel entitled his opening public lecture there, "No Religion Is an Island," calling on people from different spiritual traditions to recognize both the uniqueness of each community and their interdependence:

> The religions of the world are no more self-sufficient, no more independent, no more isolated than individuals or nations. Energies, experiences, and ideas that come to life outside the boundaries of a particular religion, or all religions, continue to challenge and to affect every religion.... *No Religion is an island....* For all the profound differences in perspective and substance, Judaism is sooner or later affected by the intellectual, moral, and spiritual events within the Christian society, and vice versa.

Heschel meeting with Augustin Cardinal Bea (right) during the Second Vatican Council, 1963 (Rabbi Marc Tannenbaum standing between them)
(Courtesy of the American Jewish Committee)

Today, many people throughout the world regard Heschel as a pioneering role model for interreligious engagement.

Perhaps the most controversial cause with which Heschel was involved was the American anti-Vietnam War movement. He was shocked to learn that the U.S. government was guilty of carrying out reckless military attacks, injuring and killing far too many innocent civilians. Many of these actions were in violation of international law. Speaking to a group of students preparing to become priests, Heschel said, "What does God demand of us primarily? Justice and compassion. What does He condemn above all? Murder, killing innocent people." And so, in 1965 he helped establish the interreligious organization Clergy and Laity Concerned About Vietnam (CALCAV) with a diverse and prominent group of colleagues, including his younger friend, the Reverend William Sloan Coffin, Jr.; Dr. King joined the group in 1967.

While Heschel and his CALCAV associates felt passionate about their work, other American religious figures opposed them, including colleagues from JTS. Some of these challengers thought that Heschel and his compatriots were simply wrong in their assessment of the behavior of the American government and armed forces. Others in the Jewish community argued that Heschel should not speak out against the American government—even if it was wrong—because it had become such a welcoming home to so many Jews. Further, the U.S. had emerged as Israel's most powerful ally. This tiny country, established only in 1948 and surrounded by several hostile neighbors, relied heavily on America's support. There were Jewish professors, politicians, and rabbis who feared that if a well-known public figure like Abraham Joshua Heschel spoke negatively about the administration in public the friendship between Jews and other Americans, and between the U.S. and Israel, might be damaged.

Heschel strongly disagreed. He felt the American government was acting unethically, and that as a loyal American citizen he needed to voice his disapproval to actions being carried out in the name of its people. One of Heschel's most famous statements about the war in Vietnam and other national issues was that "in a free society, *some* are guilty," but "*all* are responsible." We are all responsible, he said, to urge our governmental leaders—elected by the public in a democratic country—to act morally, especially in matters of life and death.

16

ISRAEL: AN ECHO OF ETERNITY

"God is no less here than there.
It is the sacred moment in which His presence is disclosed....
The history of Jerusalem is endowed with the power to inspire such moments."
—*Israel: An Echo of Eternity*, 1969

While much of Heschel's attention was focused on religious and political life in the United States, he also cared deeply about the State of Israel. He made his first visit there in 1957 to speak at an international conference on contemporary Jewish principles and values. Having recently grown a beard, Heschel joked with his close friend and colleague at JTS, Rabbi Wolfe Kelman, "How could I visit the Land of Israel without a beard!?"

Among the highlights of Heschel's time in Israel was meeting with former Israeli president Zalman Shazar, the organizer of the conference and an old friend from his Hasidic upbringing. Heschel also met with other political and religious leaders, including the first prime minister of Israel, David Ben-Gurion. Heschel returned to Israel several times and began to speak and write much more about the meaning of the Jewish state in modern life—both for the Jewish people and for humanity as a whole.

Following the 1967 war between Israel and three of its Arab neighbors—Egypt, Syria, and Jordan (commonly known as The Six-Day War, June 5-10, 1967)—Heschel penned a short book called *Israel: An Echo of Eternity* (1969). The volume was intended primarily to explain to Christians why Israel was so important to the Jewish people. In the book, he argued emphatically that Jews needed their own independent state, especially after the atrocities of the Holocaust. However, he also asserted that his people returned to their ancient ancestral homeland "not only for physical security," but also for spiritual "renewal." The subtitle of the book was intended to signal Heschel's emphasis on the importance of this land as a source of memory and inspiration. The goal, as he understood it, was for contemporary Israelis to listen deeply for the "echo" of God's voice, once heard in that very same place by the ancient prophets, and to establish a new civilization built on the eternal values of compassion and justice.

For Heschel, the land itself was not holier than other physical sites, as "God's glory fills the whole earth" (Isaiah 6:3); it held special meaning for the Jewish people because of the events that took place there. As in *The Sabbath*, Heschel focused on the power of human experience in *time* and not on objects in *space*. Relatedly, he insisted that one could cultivate a meaningful relationship with the Divine and live a rich Jewish existence both in Israel and in other countries. He encouraged the global Jewish community to view itself as interconnected.

Not surprisingly, Heschel once again faced opposition on this issue from colleagues and other public figures. Some of his associates from CALCAV, for example, were committed pacifists and felt that *all* military actions were unacceptable. Other people were critical of Israel's decision to maintain control of territories conquered in the war, as it was now ruling over many more Palestinian people living in these areas, who were also seeking independence. Heschel believed that Israel had no choice but to defend itself against the hostilities of its neighbors, and could not avoid this violent confrontation. Nonetheless, he remained hopeful that Israeli leaders would use the recent territorial gains responsibly to negotiate a peaceful and honorable solution. As he writes in the closing pages of *Israel: An Echo of Eternity*, "The choice is to live together or perish together. Let the love of life have the final word." He addressed these lines to all the parties—Arab and Israeli—involved in the conflict.

The Heschel family traveling to Israel, circa 1965
(Photograph by Lotte Jacobi; Courtesy of the Lotte Jacobi Collection, University of New Hampshire)

17

HESCHEL AND KING: FRIENDS AND RELIGIOUS ACTIVISTS

"Martin Luther King is a sign that God has not forsaken the United States of America. God has sent him to us.... I call upon every Jew to hearken to his voice, to share his vision, to follow his way."

—Rabbinical Assembly Annual Convention, Introduction of Dr. King, 1968

More than anything else, the American public came to know of Abraham Joshua Heschel through his involvement in the African American Civil Rights movement. On January 14, 1963, he gave a fiery speech at the National Conference on Religion and Race in Chicago, Illinois, organized by the National Conference of Christians and Jews. With great force, Heschel said that hating people because of the color of their skin was like suffering from "an eye disease." Racism, he insisted, clouds one's ability to see the holiness in other people. Having experienced the horrific consequences of Nazism, Heschel was determined to help stamp out racism in his new homeland.

Using his expertise as a scholar of the Hebrew Bible and his skill as a public speaker, Heschel opened his address by declaring humorously that the first conference on religion and race actually took place centuries earlier in ancient Egypt, when Moses confronted Pharaoh and demanded that he free the Israelite slaves—"Let my people go!" (Exodus 9:1). Heschel continued by stating that the ongoing struggle of African Americans to achieve true freedom and equality was clear evidence that "the outcome of that [ancient] summit meeting has not come to an end." He then challenged his audience—which included many white Jews and Christians who identified closely with the Israelite slaves—to decide if they were going to support Moses the liberator or Pharaoh the tyrant. Heschel followed this with the intentionally provocative statement that "it was easier for the Children of Israel to cross the Red Sea [Exodus 14] than for a Negro to cross certain university campuses." In so doing, he was attempting to open people's hearts to the terrible struggle young Black people faced in attempting to participate in American higher education.

It was at this historic conference that Heschel first met the Reverend Dr. Martin Luther King, Jr., the most prominent figure in the Civil Rights movement. The two men quickly became friends and together worked for justice and peace for the next several years. They shared a love of the Hebrew Bible and the teachings of the prophets, and they both believed that as religious leaders they had a responsibility to stand up for others in the name of God, especially those who were regularly mistreated and with limited power or opportunity. Both men were also exceptional speakers and writers who used their communication skills to inspire and challenge others. While Heschel and King were raised in very different environments, they were both nurtured from a young age to take on public leadership roles.

Heschel sent the following telegram to President John F. Kennedy in advance of a national meeting with religious leaders to be held the following day:

> TO PRESIDENT JOHN F. KENNEDY, THE WHITE HOUSE, JUNE 16, 1963
>
> I LOOK FORWARD TO THE PRIVILEGE OF BEING PRESENT AT MEETING TOMORROW AT 4 P.M.

> LIKELIHOOD EXISTS THAT NEGRO PROBLEM WILL BE LIKE THE WEATHER. EVERYBODY TALKS ABOUT IT BUT NOBODY DOES ANYTHING ABOUT IT. PLEASE DEMAND RELIGIOUS LEADERS' PERSONAL INVOLVEMENT NOT JUST SOLEMN DECLARATION. WE FORFEIT THE RIGHT TO WORSHIP GOD AS LONG AS WE CONTINUE TO HUMILIATE NEGROES. CHURCH, SYNAGOGUES HAVE FAILED. THEY MUST REPENT. ASK OF RELIGIOUS LEADERS TO CALL FOR NATIONAL REPENTANCE AND PERSONAL SACRIFICE. LET RELIGIOUS LEADERS DONATE ONE MONTH'S SALARY TOWARD FUNDS FOR NEGRO HOUSING AND EDUCATION. I PROPOSE THAT YOU MR. PRESIDENT DECLARE A STATE OF MORAL EMERGENCY. A MARSHALL PLAN[1] FOR AID TO NEGROES IS BECOMING A NECESSITY. THE HOUR CALLS FOR MORAL GRANDEUR AND SPIRITUAL AUDACITY.[2]

Echoing the ancient prophets, Heschel was attempting to move President Kennedy to take bold action—and to encourage religious leaders to do the same. Prayers and sermons were not enough; they had to invest concretely in the physical welfare of African Americans. While he does not mention it explicitly, Heschel also wanted the President to support the efforts of Civil Rights leaders, who were attempting to organize a national march in the nation's capital later that summer.

After much negotiation, The March on Washington for Jobs and Freedom did take place in Washington, DC on August 28, 1963. It

[1] The Marshall Plan (or the European Recovery Program) was a major U.S. financial program (1948) to help rebuild Western Europe after World War II. It was named after U.S. Secretary of State George C. Marshall, who spearheaded the initiative.

[2] Unlike with a conventional letter, one did not use full sentences or abide by the usual rules of English grammar when writing a telegram.

was at this massive protest (250,000 people) that Dr. King gave his legendary "I Have a Dream" speech. While the President was anxious about the possibility of violence and further racial division, it turned out to be a peaceful event, and is today widely viewed as a pivotal moment in the struggle for African American civil rights.

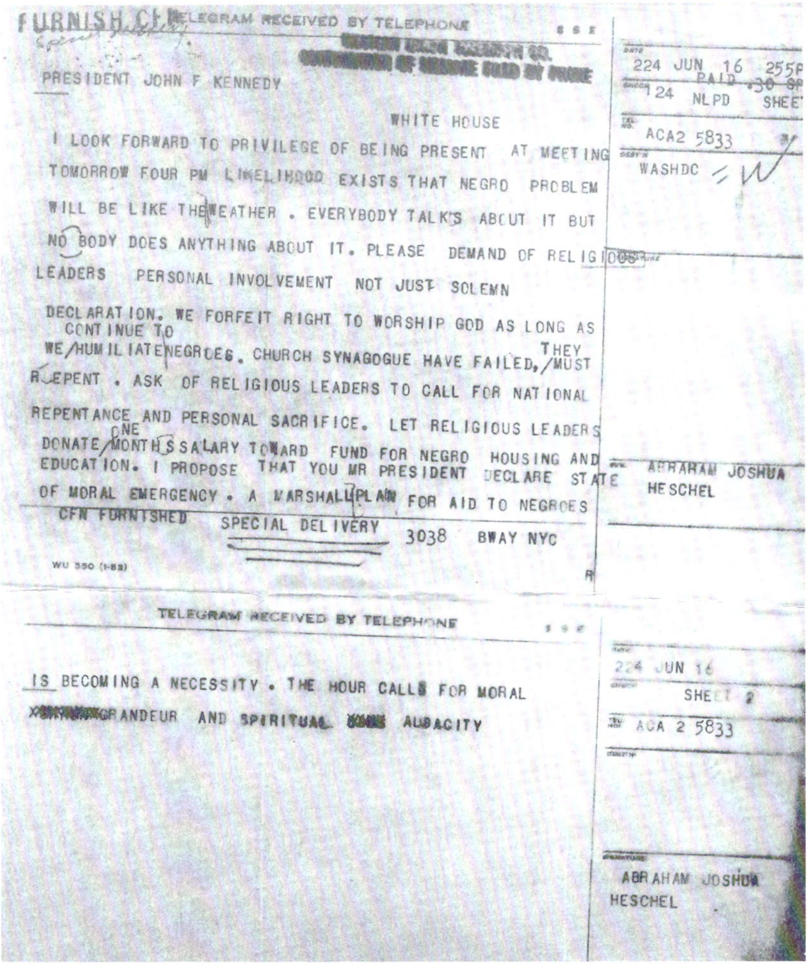

FURNISH CFN TELEGRAM RECEIVED BY TELEPHONE

224 JUN 16 255P PAID .30 SP 124 NLPD SHEET ACA2 5833 WASHDC

PRESIDENT JOHN F KENNEDY

WHITE HOUSE

I LOOK FORWARD TO PRIVILEGE OF BEING PRESENT AT MEETING TOMORROW FOUR PM LIKELIHOOD EXISTS THAT NEGRO PROBLEM WILL BE LIKE THE WEATHER . EVERYBODY TALK'S ABOUT IT BUT NO BODY DOES ANYTHING ABOUT IT. PLEASE DEMAND OF RELIGIOUS LEADERS PERSONAL INVOLVEMENT NOT JUST SOLEMN DECLARATION. WE FORFEIT RIGHT TO WORSHIP GOD AS LONG AS WE CONTINUE TO HUMILIATE NEGROES. CHURCH SYNAGOGUE HAVE FAILED, THEY MUST REPENT . ASK OF RELIGIOUS LEADERS TO CALL FOR NATIONAL REPENTANCE AND PERSONAL SACRIFICE. LET RELIGIOUS LEADERS DONATE ONE MONTH'S SALARY TOWARD FUND FOR NEGRO HOUSING AND EDUCATION. I PROPOSE THAT YOU MR PRESIDENT DECLARE STATE OF MORAL EMERGENCY . A MARSHALL PLAN FOR AID TO NEGROES

CFN FURNISHED SPECIAL DELIVERY 3038 BWAY NYC

ABRAHAM JOSHUA HESCHEL

WU 550 (1-53)

TELEGRAM RECEIVED BY TELEPHONE

224 JUN 16 SHEET 2 ACA 2 5833

IS BECOMING A NECESSITY . THE HOUR CALLS FOR MORAL GRANDEUR AND SPIRITUAL AUDACITY

ABRAHAM JOSHUA HESCHEL

Original telegram from Heschel to JFK
(Courtesy of Susannah Heschel and the Jewish Women's Archive)

In the spring of 1968, the Rabbinical Assembly of Conservative Rabbis invited Dr. King to speak at its annual convention, during which the group celebrated Heschel's sixtieth birthday. When King entered the room, the rabbis joined hands and sang the well-known gospel and protest song "We Shall Overcome" in Hebrew. In his address to this group, King said the following about his beloved rabbinic colleague:

> [Rabbi Heschel] is one of the true great men of our age.... I remember marching from Selma to Montgomery, how he stood at my side.... I remember very well when we were in Chicago for the conference on religion and race.... To a great extent, his speech inspired clergymen of all faiths...to do something they had never done before.

When Heschel returned from the famous Selma-Montgomery march, he wrote in his diary that marching with Dr. King was like walking with the great Hasidic masters from his childhood. He also stated that with every step he took along the streets of Alabama that day, he felt as if his "legs were praying"—praying for a better future for all of humankind.

When Dr. King was murdered on April 6, 1968, in Memphis, Tennessee, Heschel was heartbroken. He viewed Dr. King as a modern prophetic figure and one of the country's great leaders. Given their work together for freedom and justice, Heschel was hoping that the King family would join them later that month for the annual celebration of Passover, the Jewish holiday of freedom (marking the liberation of the ancient Israelite slaves from Egyptian bondage). Instead, at the invitation of Dr. King's grieving widow, Coretta Scott King, Heschel read a biblical passage at a memorial service for his dear friend and colleague just ten days after the Rabbinical Assembly gathering.

18

HESCHEL'S DEATH AND LEGACY

"Remember to build a life as if it were a work of art."
—*The Eternal Light* television interview, 1972

According to Jewish legend (based on Deuteronomy 34:5) Moses, the greatest of all the Hebrew prophets, left the world with a "kiss" from God. In other words, Moses died a peaceful death. Heschel, too, left this world with a kiss. After ushering in the Sabbath with the special Friday evening prayers, enjoying a festive meal, and relaxing with his family, he went to bed. He passed away in his sleep. The date was December 23, 1972 (18 *Tevet*), one week before his sixty-sixth birthday according to the Jewish calendar.

Among the last things Heschel read was an old collection of Hasidic stories and a new book about the Vietnam War. To the very end of his life, he continued his quest for compassion and justice, weaving together insights from different sources of wisdom.

After hearing of Heschel's death, a group of rabbis, priests, professors, and students came to the Heschel home to grieve with his wife Sylvia and daughter Susannah. And at the end of the first month of mourning, and again at the first anniversary of his passing, thousands of people gathered in Jewish and Christian houses of worship to study Heschel's writings and to reflect on his life. This has become an annual tradition in many communities throughout the world.

Heschel dedicated his life to serving as God's partner in improving the world. His work as a religious speaker, writer, teacher, and activist took him to synagogues and churches, schools and universities, and embassies and agencies around the globe. It also led him to develop friendships and to work in coalition with a diverse range of religious and secular people.

Although Abraham Joshua Heschel the man is no longer with us, his memory lives on through his many writings and through the efforts of his family, friends, and students, who continue to share his life and work with others. There are also thousands of people—young and old—who study and teach in schools and organizations named for him and dedicated to carrying forth his legacy. Heschel has become a revered figure in Jewish, interreligious, and interracial contexts in the United States and throughout the world.

May Abraham Joshua Heschel's memory continue to be a source of blessing, inspiration, and challenge—*Yehi zikhro barukh.*

Heschel teaching students at Jewish Theological Seminary, 1972
(Courtesy of The Jewish Theological Seminary)

MEMORIES FROM HESCHEL'S STUDENTS[1]

ESTHER H. STERN-BLOOM, PHD

My parents and my teachers at Columbia University and the Teachers Institute (now List College) of the Jewish Theological Seminary were my greatest influences. The instructors and scholars who taught me at these institutions—where I was enrolled in a combined undergraduate program of study—remain guiding lights in my life. This is not simply because of their intelligence and subject knowledge but because of their integrity, strong personalities, and *menschlikeit* (humanity). Rabbi Dr. Abraham Joshua Heschel was one of these people.

However, I was fortunate enough to be acquainted with Professor Heschel *outside* of the classroom, as I babysat for his daughter, Susannah Heschel, now an accomplished scholar, teacher, wife, and mother. One particular encounter stands out in my memory: The Heschel parents returned from an evening out, and as usual, they greeted me warmly while inquiring about my time with Susannah. Professor Heschel asked about me about my studies and my family. At some point in the conversation the discussion turned to music, which was not at all that surprising since Mrs. Sylvia Heschel was a concert pianist. Her husband also used many musical metaphors in his writings.

Standing in front of the baby grand piano in the entrance of their living room, Mrs. Heschel expressed her belief that people resemble musical instruments. She, of course, was a piano. I was flattered

---

[1] The reminiscences by rabbis Lipnick, Reimer, Weiss, and Rosenberg originally appeared in *Conservative Judaism*, Winter/Spring 1998 (honoring the twenty-fifth anniversary of Heschel's passing).

to be likened to a cello, and I cannot remember which one of us compared the quick-witted, vivacious, and bright young Susannah to a piccolo! Professor Heschel was deemed to be an organ, which Mozart considered the "king of instruments." The organ is, indeed, a complex instrument with the largest extant repertoire of any instrument in Western music. Might there still be a book to be written about Heschel and music as revealed through his poetic and lyrical style?

How blessed I am to recall this delightful personal experience with my teacher, Rabbi Dr. Abraham Joshua Heschel, and his family.

RABBI BERNARD LIPNICK (OF BLESSED MEMORY)

The incident occurred many years ago. I can never think of Professor Heschel without recalling what happened because it provides for me such a clear picture of the kind of man he was and at least one of the qualities that contributed so much to his greatness.

Heschel had arrived at our home in St. Louis late one evening after the children were asleep. He was to speak the next day at a city-wide meeting. What an honor it was to have my esteemed teacher in my home and how eager I was to spend the few minutes we had to catch up on what had transpired since we were last together.

When the hour grew late, we went to bed for a well-deserved rest. What happened the next morning, we learned about later from the professor himself.

It seems that my middle son, Daniel Adam, who was about four at the time, awakened early and discovered that someone was occupying our guest bedroom. Curious, he climbed up on the bed and, never having seen such a thing before, certainly not at such close range, began to touch the professor's luxuriant beard which was spread out over the covers. The professor awakened and was greeted with the question, "What do you need that for?" referring of course to the beard. After proper introductions, the professor and Daniel played together—the beard being by far the guest's feature which provided the greatest interest to Daniel.

Throughout that day, the two of them—the professor and the little boy—became bosom buddies, so much so that when it came time later in the day to leave for the airport, the professor lifted Daniel up for one more encounter with his beard and asked jokingly, "Daniel, do you want me to leave you my beard?" Without a moment's hesitation, Daniel shot back, "No, I'd rather have a toy!" Professor Heschel was a bit taken aback. He made some comments, kissed Daniel goodbye, and took leave of him and the rest of the family.

On the way to the airport, following a few moments of thoughtful silence, the professor said to me, "Bernie, take me to a store where I can buy a toy for Daniel." I protested that there was not enough time and that if we did, he would be in danger of missing the plane. Nothing mattered to Professor Heschel but the toy. He would have it no other way. It was to the toy store, then back to the house, where a little boy named Daniel learned firsthand that the greater the man the greater his concern for people, especially the young people of the world.

RABBI JACK REIMER

How to choose one brief story to stand for all the many that fill my mind and soul whenever I think of Dr. Heschel? Let me tell you about one brief encounter, one that lasted less than half a minute, and yet that taught me a lesson in how to look at life that I have tried to remember ever since.

I once went to a wedding. To me, it seemed like a very sad wedding. The groom and bride were both orphaned, both had physical challenges, and both were poor. There were only a few people present; there was no band, no dancing, and the refreshments were meager. All in all, it seemed like a sad event to me.

When I came back, I met Dr. Heschel in the JTS courtyard, and he asked me where I had been. I told him that I had been at a wedding, and I started to tell him why it was such a sad affair. I was halfway through my description when he interrupted me. Before I could say the words: "How sad!" he cut me off and said: "How wonderful!" And I realized that he was right. I had seen it through eyes that only noticed the sad aspects of the events. He saw it with eyes that recognized the wonder—that two lost souls, two orphans, two poor people, a couple to whom life had been so difficult—had somehow found each other and had resolved to build a life together. He saw what I hadn't seen: that the wedding was an act of faith and an occasion of joy and not a sad occasion, as I had thought.

From then on, I have tried to look at many situations in this world through his eyes. Where others could only see routine, he was able to see wonder. Where others could only see through a cynical lens, he was able to see with gratitude and appreciation. Where others could only see the world as it is, he could see an invitation to make the world *as it should be*. What wonderful *eyesight* and *insight* he had! I learned from him in that brief conversation in the courtyard that day, a conversation that could not have been more than half a minute, a whole different way of looking and of seeing that I have tried to remember and live by ever since.

RABBI GERALD B. WEISS (OF BLESSED MEMORY)

One day, in Dr. Heschel's theology class, when I was a senior student in the Rabbinical School, Dr. Heschel suddenly stopped his lecture and said, "I would like to teach you a *niggun* (melody)." He proceeded to teach us Max Helfman's composition of *Oseh Shalom* ("Maker of Peace"), his eyes closed, his voice rising with fervor at the oft-repeated word *shalom* (peace). Soon, we were all singing with him—our voices and passion for peace blending with his. One can only wonder what thought, what occurrence in his mind, his life, led to that moment—but it was a transcendent moment—one I shall remember all my days.

On reflection, it was not merely a "moment"—for I always have and always will picture him in my mind whenever I hear or sing that tune. An event became transformed into a process—a process that continues even now. I have incorporated that melody for *Oseh*

Shalom that I first learned from him into virtually every Friday evening service I have led for twenty-five years—a quarter of a century—and, whenever I sing it, I remember Rabbi Abraham Joshua Heschel (of blessed memory), my teacher, and all I was privileged to learn from his life and his lips, and that mystical moment when our voices blended in song, and our souls touched.

RABBI GERRY ROSENBERG (OF BLESSED MEMORY)

In 1961, I entered Rabbinical School. I had the privilege of working as Dr. Heschel's secretary for that year. There are many special moments that I recall with great fondness, but the most important was my admissions interview of which Dr. Heschel was a member of the committee.

Many questions were asked by the professors seated around the table. Finally, Dr. Heschel, who had remained quiet, stroking his beard, as he often did, turned to me and said, "If you were going to Alaska, what two things would you take with you?" Thinking that my answer should be appropriate for an aspiring rabbinical student, I answered, "*tallis* (prayer shawl) and *tefillin* (prayer boxes)." Dr. Heschel looked at me, and in his own, inimitable way, said, "And you wouldn't take a warm coat?"

A few moments later, he said, "What are the two most important qualities of a rabbi?" Again, trying to outmaneuver him, I answered, "A desire to serve and self-confidence to be able to serve." This time, Dr. Heschel looked at me and said, "Remember this: too much self-confidence is a modern form of idolatry, while confidence in God is an eternal virtue."

That was the end of my interview, but those words never left me. The influence of Dr. Heschel touched all of us who were privileged to be in his presence.

RABBI NAAMAH KELMAN

My father, Rabbi Wolfe Kelman, had a special relationship with Rabbi Dr. Abraham Joshua Heschel. They met at the Jewish Theological

Seminary in 1945, where Heschel just joined the faculty, and my father was an incoming rabbinical school student. My father was considering dropping out; his classmate, Samuel Dresner, suggested that he meet with Heschel before doing so. That meeting, which included the realization that they were both refugees from Hasidic dynasties—lost and found at JTS—launched a close, decades-long, friendship and partnership.

At the time, we had only one telephone in our home (like most other people we knew). When I picked up Heschel's calls, he would ask in his soft, lilting voice, "Is your fah-ther there?" Years later, after I had read several of Heschel's books and understood his greatness, I wondered which father he had in mind?! But he never promoted his "greatness" with me or my family. In fact, he usually spoke in an unassuming manner.

Heschel's words echoed deeply and powerfully in his writings, but in person he was a gentle presence. There was for many years a wonderful portrait of him in the Heschel family living room on Riverside Drive overlooking the Hudson River. In it, he stands in the wilderness, barefoot, wearing a simple black academic robe. It is startling to behold a scholar-prophet humbly leading us through the wilderness.

Upon ordination, my father became the director of the Rabbinical Assembly of Conservative rabbis; his office was at JTS. And so, he often picked up Professor Heschel (that is what he always called him) from his office to walk home. Leaving the Seminary, they walked to the Heschels' apartment, park side, on 115th Street. Heschel would then say, "Let me walk you home Wolfe." When they reached our apartment on 101st Street my father would reciprocate: "Now let me walk you home!" Back and forth, schmoozing about personal matters and deliberating over the future of the Jewish people, they walked. Heschel was kind enough to tell me how much he valued my father's "wise counsel"; my father revered Abraham Joshua Heschel, even when they disagreed. As a witness to this unique relationship, I learned a great deal about companionship, a shared passion for Jewish life, love, hope, and repair.

AFTERWORD

The photograph (see front cover) of Rabbi Dr. Abraham Joshua Heschel walking arm-in-arm with the Reverend Dr. Martin Luther King, Jr., and other African American Civil Rights leaders in the march from Selma to Montgomery, Alabama (1965), has become iconic in interreligious and interracial circles. For many of us, it symbolizes the transformative possibilities of allyship across difference. When one learns about the close relationship Rabbi Heschel and Dr. King developed through the work for justice and compassion, the image of them engaging together in this sacred act of non-violent protest becomes even more powerful. While these men came from very different backgrounds, they were united in their commitment to a vision of life in which all human beings are treated with dignity and given the opportunity to fulfill their highest aspirations. Like the prophets of old, Heschel and King understood that to call themselves religious leaders meant that they had to serve as God's partners in the global project of redemption.

As a pastor, educator, and public servant, I have attempted in my own ways to follow in the footsteps of these renowned American spiritual and ethical models. Reading about their triumphs and struggles helps to inspire and challenge me to become my best self—publicly and privately. This requires honest reflection about my strengths, passions, limitations, and growth edges. As Rabbi Heschel taught us, we must seek to live as both "inheritors" and "innovators," listening carefully to the wisdom of our forebearers and to our inner voices. Each of us is, in the words of this modern sage, a "novelty," not a "mere repetition or extension of the past" or an "anticipation of things to come."

I pray that this wonderful book about one of the great Jewish scholars and social activists of the past century helps younger readers actualize their unique, God-given, talents and join in ongoing efforts to establish a more compassionate, just, and sustainable world.

The Honorable Reverend Dr. Suzan Johnson-Cook
United States Ambassador-at-Large for International Religious Freedom
Obama Administration

Heschel (right) with Coretta Scott King (widow of Dr. King), Rev. William Sloane Coffin (back left), and Pastor Richard John Neuhaus, outside of the Metropolitan African Methodist Episcopal Church, Washington, DC, 1969
(Photograph by John Goodwin; Courtesy of David and Benjamin Goodwin)

KEY HEBREW AND YIDDISH TERMS

Ba'al Shem Tov: Hebrew for "Master of the Good Name"; a Jewish mystical folk healer. Israel ben Eliezer was the most famous such healer, and is the first great figure in Hasidic lore.

Hasid (*Hasidim*, plural): Hebrew for "devout one"; a follower of the Ba'al Shem Tov and the Hasidic masters since the eighteenth century.

hesed: Hebrew for "lovingkindness," "compassion," or "mercy."

illui: Hebrew for "prodigy."

Kabbalah: "That which is received" or "The Receiving"; the Jewish mystical tradition.

Kaddish: Hebrew for "sanctified"; the traditional memorial prayer for the dead.

kadosh: Hebrew for "holy," as in the Sabbath.

kavannah: Hebrew and for "intention" or "focus."

kvitel (*kvitelah*, plural): Yiddish for "note"—prayer slip Hasidic Jews and others give to their spiritual leaders.

makom kadosh: Hebrew for "holy place"—usually a reference to a place used for prayer or study.

mamme loshen: Yiddish for "mother tongue" or native language.

menschlikeit: Yiddish for "humanity"—the word *mensch* means a person.

minyan: Hebrew for a "prayer group" of ten or more Jewish adults (in traditional communities, men).

niggun: Hebrew for "melody"—often a wordless melody.

Ohev Yisrael: Hebrew for "One Who Loves the People of Israel"; an informal title given to Rabbi Abraham Joshua Heschel of Apt.

p'sak: Jewish legal "ruling."

rebbe (*rebbeim*, plural): Yiddish for "rabbi" or "master"—the title given to Hasidic leaders.

Shabbos (or *Shabbat*): Hebrew for "Sabbath."

Shalom aleikhem: Hebrew for "Peace be upon you"—a common greeting in Jewish circles.

Shoah: Hebrew for "Catastrophe"—an alternative term for the Holocaust.

shteibel: Yiddish for a small, informal synagogue/study hall.

Talmud: Hebrew for "Instruction"—the name of the foundational work of ancient Rabbinic Jewish thought—including theology, ethics, and ritual practice.

tateh: Yiddish for "father."

tefilah: Hebrew for "prayer."

tisch: Yiddish for "table"—a gathering at the table of a Hasidic master on the Sabbath or holidays.

Torah: Hebrew for "Teaching"; it can refer to the Five Books of Moses—Genesis, Exodus, Leviticus, Numbers, and Deuteronomy (*Pentateuch* in Greek)—the Hebrew Bible as a whole, or both, along with the many Jewish teachings that flow from these foundational texts.

tzaddeket: Hebrew for "righteous women"—the male form is *tzaddik.*

tzedakah: Hebrew for "just (*tzedek*) giving"—financial support for the needy.

yarmulke: Yiddish for "head covering"; in Hebrew, a *kippah*.

yeshiva: Hebrew for "sitting"—the name for a traditional Jewish academy.

zeide: Yiddish for "grandfather" or elder.

Abraham Joshua Heschel, 1907-1972
(Photograph by Joel Orent; Courtesy of Dror Bondi)

A TIMELINE OF ABRAHAM JOSHUA HESCHEL'S LIFE

1907 – Born in Warsaw, Poland

1925 – Leaves Warsaw for Vilna, Lithuania for high school

1927 – Moves to Berlin, Germany, for university

1933 – Publishes his first book: a collection of Yiddish poetry, *Human: God's Ineffable Name* (*Der Shem ha'Meforash: Mensch*)

1935 – Graduates from the University of Berlin as a Doctor of Philosophy

1938 – Expelled from Frankfurt, Germany, back to Warsaw, Poland

1939 – Leaves Warsaw for the United States, via London, England

1940 – Arrives in the United States to teach at the Hebrew Union College (HUC) in Cincinnati, Ohio

1945 – Moves to New York City to teach at The Jewish Theological Seminary (JTS)

1946 – Marries Sylvia Straus in Los Angeles, California

1950 – Publishes first book in English: *The Earth Is the Lord's*: *The Inner World of the Jew in Eastern Europe*

1952 – Susannah (Channa Shoshanah) Heschel is born to Sylvia and Abraham Joshua Heschel

1952 – Publishes *God in Search of Man: A Philosophy of Judaism*

1962 – Publishes *The Prophets*, based on his doctoral thesis from the University of Berlin

1962-65 – Serves as a special advisor to the Second Vatican Council, convened by Pope John XXIII, then continued by Pope Paul VI

1963 – Speaks at the First Conference on Race and Religion in Chicago, Illinois, where he meets the Reverend Dr. Martin Luther King, Jr.

1965 – Marches for African American voting rights with Dr. King and others from Selma to Montgomery, Alabama

1967 – Publishes *Israel: An Echo of Eternity*

1972 – Abraham Joshua Heschel dies at age sixty-five

SUGGESTIONS FOR FURTHER LEARNING

BOOKS BY ABRAHAM JOSHUA HESCHEL (A SELECTION)

Human: God's Ineffable Name [Yiddish original, 1933], translation by Zalman M. Schachter-Shalomi (Albion-Andalus Books, 2015).

The Earth Is the Lord's: The Inner World of the Jew in Eastern Europe (Jewish Lights Publishing, 1949).

The Sabbath: Its Meaning for Modern Man (Farrar, Straus and Giroux, 1951).

Man's Quest for God: Studies in Prayer and Symbolism (Charles Scribner's Sons, 1954).

God in Search of Man: A Philosophy of Judaism (Farrar, Straus and Giroux, 1955).

The Insecurity of Freedom: Essays on Human Existence (Farrar, Straus and Giroux, 1955).

The Prophets (Harper and Row, 1962).

Israel: An Echo of Eternity (Farrar, Straus and Giroux, 1969).

COLLECTIONS OF HESCHEL'S WRITINGS

Moral Grandeur and Spiritual Audacity: Essays, edited by Susannah Heschel (Farrar, Straus and Giroux, 1997).

I Asked for Wonder: A Spiritual Anthology, edited with an introduction by Samuel H. Dresner (Crossroad Publishing, 2010).

Abraham Joshua Heschel: Essential Writings, selected with an introduction by Susannah Heschel (Orbis Books, 2011).

Thunder in the Soul: To Be Known by God, edited by Robert Erlewine, foreword by Susannah Heschel (Plough Publishing, 2021).

BOOKS AND FILM ON HESCHEL BY OTHERS

Naomi Pasachoff, *Great Jewish Thinkers: Their Lives and Work* [for teen and young adult readers] (Behrman House, 1990).

Or N. Rose, *Abraham Joshua Heschel: Man of Spirit, Man of Action* [for readers ages 9-12] (Jewish Publication Society, 2003).

Richard Michelson, *As Good as Anybody: Martin Luther King, Jr., and Abraham Joshua Heschel's Amazing March Toward Freedom* [for readers ages 6-9] (Dragonfly Books, 2013).

Edward K. Kaplan, *Abraham Joshua Heschel: Mind, Heart, and Soul* [a scholarly biography] (Jewish Publication Society, 2019).

Martin Doblmeier, "Spiritual Audacity: The Abraham Joshua Heschel Story" [documentary film] (Journey Films, 2021).

Julien E. Zelizer, *Abraham Joshua Heschel: A Life of Radical Amazement* [a scholarly biography] (Yale University Press, 2021).

ACKNOWLEDGMENTS

We wish to thank the following individuals and institutions for their help and support:

Tali Anisfeld
Dr. Dror Bondi
Rafi Ellenson
Peter Geffen
Dr. Susannah Heschel
Rabbi Dr. Morey Hoberman
Dr. Celene Ibrahim
Gideon Israel
Marvin Israelow
Dr. Edward Kaplan (of blessed memory) and Jana Kaplan
Andrew Katz
David Mahfouda
Rabbi Dr. Michael Marmur
Andy Offit and Suzanne Offit
Kim Pimley
Dr. Eboo Patel
Colin Rolfe
Dr. Judith Rosenbaum
Reverend Robert Schenck
Marilyn Stern
Jon M. Sweeney
Carol Targum and Lucy Targum
Reverend Adam Russell Taylor
Rabbi Yehuda DovBer Zirkind

* * *

The Miller Center of Hebrew College
Interfaith America
The Library of The Jewish Theological Seminary
Paris Lodron University of Salzburg

INDEX

Pages numbers in **boldface** refer to photographs.

OTHER NEW JEWISH BOOKS FROM MONKFISH

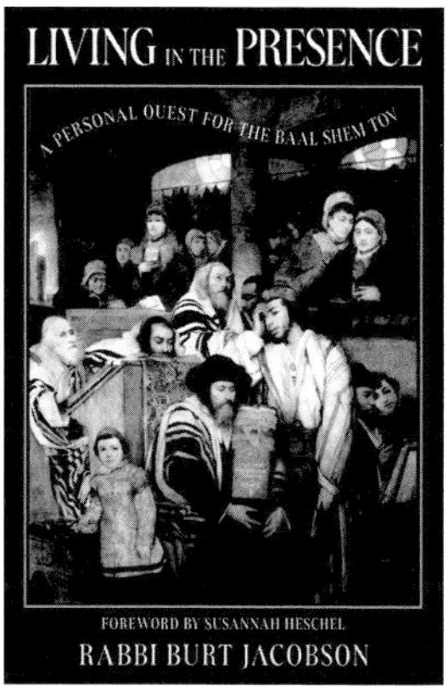

LIVING IN THE PRESENCE: A PERSONAL QUEST FOR THE BAAL SHEM TOV **RABBI BURT JACOBSON**

A rabbi's lifelong journey to discover the source and inspiration of Hasidism.

"Burt has striven his entire life to hand over the legacy of Hasidism and of my father to generations to come. Let us listen to his voice in the pages of this book so that we may be enriched by our Hasidic inheritance and offer that heritage as a great fire of passionate devotion to God, to one another, to our fragile earth to generations to come." —**Susannah Heschel**

ZEN MIND, JEWISH MIND: KOAN, MIDRASH, AND THE LIVING WORD **RAMI SHAPIRO**

The questioning perennial beginner is central to both Zen and Jewish. Rabbi Rami demonstrates a daring, iconoclastic, often humorous mind devoted to shattering the words, texts, isms, and ideologies on which expert mind—closed to inquiry—depends.

"A great way to deepen your spiritual life is to take a deep dive into a tradition other than your own—especially if you have a competent guide, and Rabbi Rami is an extraordinary guide. Not into Zen? Not a Jew? Not a problem. Anyone on any path will benefit enormously from this profoundly illuminating book." —**Philip Goldberg**, author of *American Veda*

WEDDING AT THE GRAVEYARD AND OTHER TALES OF THE JEWISH FANTASTICAL **NILTON BONDER**

A Romanian woman, resident of Copacabana, wants to marry her dead fiancé. The discovery of a manuscript from the Inquisition, written to defame a woman, has the power to awaken lust and perversion in whomever reads it. A boy who scares his parents with paranormal powers prepares for his bar mitzvah.

"Rabbi Nilton Bonder presents a lucid and rich encounter of paranormal situations through a range of captivating and unforgettable short stories, including his own offering, that are sure to haunt and enchant the reader." —**Rabbi Marc Schneier**, Hampton Synagogue; author of *Sons of Abraham*, with a foreword by President Bill Clinton

AVAILABLE FROM BOOKSELLERS EVERYWHERE

MONKFISH BOOK PUBLISHING • RHINEBECK, NEW YORK • MONKFISHPUBLISHING.COM